CU00839370

CONTEMPORARY GER

PETER SCHNEIDER

Series Editor

Rhys W. Williams has been Professor of German and Head of the German Department at University of Wales, Swansea, since 1984. He has published extensively on the literature of German Expressionism and on the post-war novel. He is Director of the Centre for Contemporary German Literature at University of Wales, Swansea.

CONTEMPORARY GERMAN WRITERS

Series Editor: Rhys W. Williams

PETER SCHNEIDER

edited by

Colin Riordan

CARDIFF
UNIVERSITY OF WALES PRESS
1995

© The Contributors, 1995

British Library Cataloguing-in-Publication Data
A catalogue record for this book is available from the British Library.

ISBN 0-7083-1289-6

All rights reserved. No part of this book may be reproduced, stored in a retrieval system, or transmitted, in any form or by any means, electronic, mechanical, photocopying, recording or otherwise, without clearance from the University of Wales Press, 6 Gwennyth Street, Cardiff, CF2 4YD.

Cover design by Olwen Fowler, Pentan Design Practice, Cardiff.
Printed in Great Britain by Dinefwr Press, Llandybie.

Contents

List of Contributors

R. M. Gillett is Lecturer in German at Queen Mary and Westfield College, University of London. He is a specialist in modern German literature, with a particular interest in the works of Hubert Fichte.

Duncan Large is Lecturer in German at the University of Wales, Swansea. In 1993 he published a translated edition of Sarah Kofman's *Nietzsche and Metaphor*; he has recently completed a new translation of Nietzsche's *Twilight of the Idols* and is working on a study of Musil's *Der Mann ohne Eigenschaften*.

Stephan Reinhardt (Heidelberg) is a broadcaster, editor and literary critic. He reviews extensively for the press and radio; among his most recent publications is the acclaimed biography of Alfred Andersch.

Colin Riordan is Senior Lecturer in German at the University of Wales, Swansea. He is the author of a book and several articles on Uwe Johnson. In 1993 he edited Peter Schneider's *Vati* with an introduction and notes for Manchester University Press.

Rhys W. Williams is Professor of German at the University of Wales, Swansea. He has published extensively on German Expressionism (Sternheim, Benn, Einstein, Kaiser and Toller) and on contemporary literature (Andersch, Böll, Lenz and Walser).

Preface

Contemporary German Writers

Each volume of the Contemporary German Writers series is devoted to an author who has spent a period as Visiting Writer at the Centre for Contemporary German Literature in the Department of German at the University of Wales, Swansea. The first chapter in each volume contains an original, previously unpublished piece by the writer concerned; the second consists of a biographical sketch, outlining the main events of the author's life and setting the works in context, particularly for the non-specialist or general reader. A third chapter will, in each case, contain an interview with the author, normally conducted during the writer's stay in Swansea. Subsequent chapters will contain contributions by invited British and German academics and critics on aspects of the writer's *œuvre*. While each volume will seek to provide both an overview of the author and some detailed analysis of individual works, the nature of that critical engagement will inevitably depend on the relative importance of the author concerned and on the amount of critical material which his or her work has previously inspired. Each volume includes an extensive bibliography designed to fill any gaps or remedy deficiencies in existing bibliographies. The intention is to produce in each case a book which will serve both as an introduction to the writer concerned and as a resource for specialists in contemporary German literature.

Peter Schneider

The present volume opens with a contribution by Peter Schneider himself, consisting of an earlier, and ultimately discarded, version of the first three chapters of his novel *Paarungen* (1992). After the brief biographical sketch, the remaining chapters are intended as far as possible to fill gaps in previous research on Schneider. The *Gespräch* in Chapter Three explores a range of topics, including discussion of hitherto neglected works such as *Totoloque* and *Ratte – tot*, and matters of general interest, such as Schneider's attitude to feminism. Stephan Reinhardt's contribution in Chapter Four offers a critical résumé of the writer's political development between 1964 and 1994, while Rhys W. Williams offers a reappraisal of *Lenz*, underlining, among other things, the importance of Maoist notions of political activism for an understanding of the text. Schneider's collection of short stories *Die Wette* is the subject of R. M. Gillett's critical analysis, a chapter which seeks to place the stories within the context of Schneider's other works, particularly his essays. Colin Riordan's chapter on *Paarungen* offers the first essay-length appraisal of Schneider's latest fictional work. If no chapter is devoted exclusively to *Der Mauerspringer* (although both Stephan Reinhardt and R. M. Gillett touch on the work) it is because of the relatively large number of published essays already devoted to this text, details of which may be found in the second section of the bibliography. The extensive first section of the bibliography, on the primary works, offers, to the best of our knowledge, the most exhaustive list currently available and is thus an invaluable resource for future researchers.

Abbreviations

Full bibliographical details appear in Chapter 8.

AN	*Ansprachen* (2nd edn., 1981)
AP	*Atempause* (1977)
BP	*Die Botschaft des Pferdekopfs* (1981)
DÄ	*Deutsche Ängste* (1988)
DMS	*Der Mauerspringer* (1982)
DW	*Die Wette* (1978)
EM	*Extreme Mittellage* (1990)
EMR	*Extreme Mittellage* (revised edn., 1992)
L	*Lenz* (1973)
MK	*Messer im Kopf* (1979)
P	*Paarungen* (1992)
RT	*Ratte – tot* (1985)
T	*Totoloque* (1985)
V	*Vati* (1987)
VEG	*Vom Ende der Gewißheit* (1994)
VF	*. . . schon bist du ein Verfassungsfeind* (1975)

1

Anfänge

PETER SCHNEIDER

Es handelt sich um die drei Anfangskapitel einer früheren Version des Romans Paarungen, *die ich aus formalen Gründen für die endgültige Fassung verworfen habe.*

I: Stadtführung

Damals war die Stadt vor allem wegen ihrer Mauer berühmt. Einem Gerücht nach, das vor allem die Reisebranche belebte, war es in der Stadt unmöglich, eine halbe Stunde geradeaus zu gehen, ohne auf eine Mauer zu stoßen bzw. an eine Mauer zu denken. Die Stadtväter hatten lange gezögert, die touristische Hauptattraktion in den amtlichen Werbebroschüren zu verzeichnen. Denn das bei weitem bekannteste Bauwerk der Stadt verdankte seinen Ruf nicht seiner Schönheit. Die Mauer bestach den Besucher weder durch ihr Alter (22 Jahre), noch durch ihre Höhe (2,70 m), noch durch ihre Bauweise (Fertigteile aus Zementeisengemisch). Nicht einmal hinsichtlich ihrer Länge (167 Kilometer) konnte sie es mit vergleichbaren Unternehmen – dem römischen Limes oder der chinesischen Mauer – aufnehmen. Einzigartig an der Mauer war der Umstand, daß sie, statt außen herumzulaufen, die Stadt in der Mitte durchteilte und die östliche Hälfte der Stadt von der westlichen hermetisch abriegelte.

Für den Ortsunkundigen war es dennoch nicht einfach, das Ziel seiner Reise ausfindig zu machen. Wer sich abseits von den Kolonnen der Reisebusse auf den Weg machte, verlief sich leicht zwischen den zahlreichen Brandmauern und Hinterhofmauern der Stadt. Snobisten zogen diesen Mauerwildwuchs der staatlich

betreuten Grenzmauer sogar vor. Der alternative Reisende entdeckte Kinderspielplätze, von mannshohen Mauern umstellt.
Straßencafés im Schatten von Brandmauern, deren Echo das Klirren
eines Kaffeelöffels zum Kirchengeläut verstärkte. Stark gesicherte,
turnhallengroße Hinterhöfe, die durch weitere, Trennmauern in
Isolierzellen für jeweils einen Ahorn zergliedert waren. Parkplätze
vor fünfstöckigen, fensterlosen Ziegelwänden, in deren Mitte
manchmal, hinter einem versteckten Toilettenfenster, ein Licht aufleuchtete und ein geheimnisvolles Innenleben verriet.

Falls der Reisende am Ende seines Stadtbummels doch noch die
Muttermauer erreichte und einen der Aussichtstürme bestieg, die
dort zu Schauzwecken aufgestellt waren, war er in aller Regel
enttäuscht. Denn das Original erreichte an keiner Stelle die Höhe,
die es in der Phantasie des Betrachters einnahm. Es wirkte eher wie
die Billigausführung eines architektonischen Leitmotivs, das sich
erst im Zentrum der Stadt voll entfaltet hatte. Vor dem inneren
Auge des Reisenden formte sich das Bild einer Stadt, die sich
gleichsam von den Rändern gegen das Zentrum ausdehnt, einem
Programm der Zellteilung folgend, das ein Wachstum aus-
schließlich nach innen, durch fortwährendes Teilen und Stückeln
gestattet. Am seltsamsten war, daß die Einwohner ihren Mauertick
nicht zu bemerken schienen. Es war, als führten sie mit ihrem
rastlosen Trennen und Teilen eine Zeichnung aus, die in ihrer Seele
eingegraben war.

Reisende, die die empfohlene Aufenthaltsdauer von zwei Tagen
überschritten, berichteten von einer zweiten Eigentümlichkeit der
Stadt, die Herz und Verstand ihrer Zuhörer herausforderte. Einige
erzählten von einem Fluch, andere sprachen von einem Virus,
wieder andere fabulierten von einem Drachen, der die Stadt
tyrannisiere. In einem Punkt trafen sich alle Gerüchte: einem
unerforschten Gesetz folgend lösten sich alle Liebesbeziehungen,
gleichgültig, ob sie als wilde oder standesamtliche Ehen geführt
wurden, nach spätestens zwei Jahren auf. Statistiker und Sozio-
logen, die in aller Stille anreisten, erfaßten das Phänomen zahlen-
mäßig, ohne es erklären zu können. Ihre Erhebungen ergaben, daß
eine Paarbeziehung in der westlichen Halbstadt eine durch-
schnittliche Lebenserwartung von einem Jahr, 278 Tagen und drei
Stunden hat. Fallstudien zeigten, daß dieser Mittelwert nur durch
einige Außenbezirke gehalten wurde, in denen sich Reste eines
Arbeitermilieus behauptet hatten. Auch die ungewöhnlich hohe
Anzahl von Rentnern und Angehörigen des öffentlichen Dienstes

wirkte sich offenbar stabilisierend aus. Unstreitig war aber auch, daß dieser Mittelwert durch das Treiben im Zentrum der Stadt, rechts und links ihrer öden Prachtstraße, tendenziell nach unten gedrückt wurde. Hier waren es vor allem die Dreißig- bis Vierzigjährigen beiderlei Geschlechts, die für einen weiteren Verfall sorgten. Die Prognose verschlechterte sich noch, wenn man bedachte, daß sich das Künstler-, Schwarzarbeiter- und Studenten-völkchen, das sich dort tummelte, durch einen unablässigen Zustrom vergrößerte. Die letzte Volkszählung erklärte vor allem die Gründe für den in der Stadt besonders populären Volks-zählungsboykott: in keiner Stadt der Welt, New York vielleicht ausgenommen, hatte jene Bevölkerungsgruppe, die von Stipendien, Sozialhilfe, Schwarzarbeit und Gelegenheitsdiebstählen lebt, ein vergleichbares Ausmaß erreicht. Dieser als »Minderheiten« ver-harmlosten Gruppe war es wohl zu verdanken, daß das mittlere Durchhaltevermögen aller erfaßten Liebespaare von Jahr zu Jahr weiter absank.

An dieser Stelle verlasse ich die Welt der Fragebögen und Hochrechnungen und greife auf ein Verfahren zurück, das den Sozialforschern als ein steinzeitliches Mittel zur Erkundung des Liebesverhaltens gilt: die Rede ist vom Erzählen. Die Mängel des Verfahrens sind bekannt: es wird selbst bescheidenen wissen-schaftlichen Ansprüchen nicht gerecht. Denn der Geschichten-erzähler erkennt keinen Durchschnittsfall an, er geht von der Einzigartigkeit jeder Geschichte aus. Seine Daten lassen sich nicht verifizieren, da er Authentisches und Erfundenes unentwirrbar vermischt. Von ihm ist auch kein bündiges Untersuchungsergebnis zu erwarten. Er hat zwar hin und wieder eine Hypothese im Kopf, vergißt sie aber meist im Lauf der Erzählung irgendeinem Detail zuliebe. Er steckt kein repräsentatives Stadtviertel ab: als Ort der Handlung genügt ein einziger Kneipentisch, der im Frühling höchstwahrscheinlich auf dem Straßentrottoir steht.

April, früher Nachmittag. In der zementgrauen geschlossenen Wolkendecke, die seit Wochen den Himmel bedeckt, zeigen sich erste Risse. Die Wolken, bleischwer von den Auspuff- und Schornsteinemissionen sonnenarmer Tage, brauchen zur Zeit etwa eine Stunde, um sich von einer Fernsehantenne bis zur nächsten zu bewegen. Von der nahegelegenen Prachtstraße dringt das Grund-geräusch eines nie anhaltenden Autostroms, aus dem, mit aufheulenden Motoren, vereinzelte Abbieger ausscheren und die verkehrsberuhigte Seitenstraße als Slalomrennstrecke benutzen. In

dem Augenblick, da die Wolkendecke über dem roten Ziegeldach
der Nummer 15 ein erstes Lichtbündel durchläßt, rückt der Kellner
aus dem Restaurant »Tent« einen Plastiktisch in den Sonnenfleck
auf dem Trottoir. Für einen Augenblick verschwindet er wieder
hinter dem spiegelnden Fenster. Als er mit einem weißen Tuch auf
dem Arm zurückkehrt, hat sich der Lichtfleck um mehrere Meter
verschoben. Ohne zu zögern folgt der Kellner den Anweisungen
der Sonne und rückt Tisch und drei Stühle an die bezeichnete
Stelle. Das wird er noch mehrmals tun und erst aufgeben, als der
Lichtfleck auf die gegenüberliegende Straßenseite abwandert.

II: Auftritt Marina

Um diese Zeit suchte, von der Prachtstraße kommend, eine
auffällige Erscheinung den Weg ins »Tent«. Auffällig war nicht nur
das Ticktack der Stöckelschuhe – ein Signal, das in der vom
Geschlechterkampf gezeichneten Stadt nur noch selten zu hören
war. Bei jedem Schritt schlugen smaragdgrüne Perlenschnüre, die
in Dutzende von schwarzen Haarzöpfchen geflochten waren, an
tellergroße Ohrgehänge. Was die männlichen Passanten, die hier
wie überall in der Stadt ihr erotisches Interesse meist nur noch
durch aggressives Wegschauen bekundeten, verstört aufblicken ließ,
war die Hautfarbe des farbenprächtigen Geschöpfs: kaffee-,
kastanien-, eichenholzbraun – keine Wortverbindung traf es ganz.
Wahrscheinlich entsprach diese Mischfarbe ziemlich exakt jenem
Durchschnittswert, den die Weltbevölkerung bei entschlossener
Durchmischung erreichen würde. Nach den Berechnungen der
Statistiker kommen auf einen Teil Weiß neun Teile Farbig, und der
weiße Farbteil ist weiter im Sinken begriffen. Deswegen verdankte
die Erscheinung ihre Auffälligkeit eigentlich nur dem Umstand,
daß sich die Einwohner der Stadt so erstaunlich weiß erhalten
hatten.

Im Unterschied zu ihren Bewunderern war Marina sich über die
Bedingungen ihrer Wirkung volkommen klar. Sie genoß es sogar,
in diesem absurd weißen Erdteil für ein Merkmal bestaunt zu
werden, das in anderen Weltregionen niemand bemerkte, und war
entschlossen, ihren Überraschungsvorteil zu nutzen. Sie wußte
auch, daß der neugierige Blick der paar Männer, die sich aus dem
Augenspiel der Geschlechter noch nicht gänzlich verabschiedet
hatten, vor allem ihrer Hautfarbe galt. Keiner von ihnen hätte sie

an einer Bushaltestelle in Rio de Janeiro oder New York wiedererkannt. Die Aufmerksamkeit, die sie hier erregte, verdankte sie wohl vor allem einer restriktiven Ausländerpolitik. Aber Neugier, auch wenn sie auf bloßen Mangel zurückging, war einstweilen angenehmer als Überdruß – warum sollte sie ihr kleines Privileg nicht in Anspruch nehmen?

Wir haben es offenbar nicht nur mit einer auffälligen, sondern auch mit einer klugen und unerschrockenen Person zu tun. Einer Männerlegende zufolge galt körperliche Unscheinbarkeit damals noch als eine unerläßliche Bedingung für weibliche Intelligenz, mit der Folge, daß Männer auf Frauen, in denen sich Schönheit mit Bildung und wissenschaftlicher Schärfe paarte, nicht vorbereitet waren. Aus diesem Grund hätte niemand der auffälligen Erscheinung das Forschungsprojekt zugetraut, das sie von der Stanford University direkt ins »Tent« führte. Dort hatte sie eine gelehrte Komission mit einem 12 Seiten–Exposé für ein ungewöhnliches Projekt gewonnen. Nachdem europäische Wissenschaftler jahrhundertelang die Kultur der sogenannten Naturvölker erkundet hatten, sei es höchste Zeit, die Blickrichtung umzukehren. Marina Cuauthemok vom Stamm der Nahua hatte die Absicht, das Liebesleben mitteleuropäischer Männer ethnologisch zu erforschen.

Sie nahm, ohne die Zustimmung des Kellners abzuwarten, an einem der freien Tische Platz, bestellte ein Mineralwasser und holte einen Schreibblock und einen Kugelschreiber aus ihrer Umhängetasche. Tisch und Restaurant trug sie maßstabgerecht in eine Lageskizze ein, in der bereits zahlreiche andere Orte verzeichnet waren. Aus der Sicht dieser Skizze war das Zentrum der Stadt ein einziger riesiger Gaststättenbetrieb, in dem nur die Namen von Restaurants und Tischnummern eine Orientierung erlaubten. Das Viereck, das Marina jetzt zeichnete, war vorläufig leer wie der Tisch, den es meinte. Als der Kellner dem ungewöhnlichen Gast eine Flasche Pellegrino hinstellte, sah er den geschmückten Kopf über ein Buch gebeugt, auf dessen Titelseite zu lesen stand: Die Serapionsbrüder. Einer der perlengeschmückten Zöpfe warf, wie ein Lesezeichen, einen Schatten auf die Schrift des romantischen Dichters.

III: Ankünfte

1

Eduard erwachte durch den Stich eines Zeigefingers in seine linke
Schulter. Eine weibliche Stimme sprach mit routinierter Sanftheit in
sein Ohr, eine Hand drückte auf einen Knopf unter seinem
Ellbogen. Durch das Vorschnellen der Rückenlehne, dem Eduard
im Halbschlaf mit einer Beugung des Oberkörpers folgte, rutschte
ein Notizbuch von seinen Knien. Als er sich danach bückte, sackte
das Flugzeug plötzlich stark ab, Eduard wurde von einem Schwin-
del erfaßt. Vergeblich versuchte er sich, mit dem Kopf zwischen
den Beinen, an die Durchsage der Lautsprecherstimme zu erinnern.
Stattdessen hallte ein Satz in seinen Ohren nach, von dem er nicht
wußte, ob er ihn vor dem Einschlafen notiert oder im Traum gehört
hatte: »du kannst nämlich gar nicht lieben«. Als er das Büchlein
unter dem Vordersitz hervorgezogen und sich angeschnallt hatte,
war ihm, als hätte er es aus 1000 Meter Tiefe zurückgeholt.

Eduard sah sich um. Einige Passagiere an den Fensterseiten
hatten ihre Fotoapparate hervorgezogen und knipsten den Dunst
vor den Fenstern. Von hinten patschte eine Kinderhand auf
Eduards Kopf, krallte sich dann, von dem kichernden Tadel der
Eltern eher ermuntert, an seinen Haaren fest. Wütend überlegte
Eduard, warum er seit einiger Zeit immer in die Nähe von zwei-
bis fünfjährigen Passagieren gesetzt wurde. Jedesmal, wenn er jetzt
flog, sank der Kopf eines neben ihm sitzenden Kindes auf seinen
Arm, wippende Kinderbeine traten ihm in die Waden, Kinder-
stimmchen brüllten, ohne je Atem zu holen, ihr hohes C in sein
Ohr. Früher waren ihm solche Belästigungen entweder erspart
geblieben oder er hatte sie nicht wahrgenommen. Seit einiger Zeit
aber wurde er, als vollkommen Unschuldiger, an einem Gattungs-
schicksal beteiligt, das er bisher erfolgreich vermieden hatte.

Als das Räderwerk ausgefahren wurde, sah Eduard Rauch-
wolken aus einem der vorderen Sitze aufsteigen. Eine Stewardeß
redete auf den rauchenden Fahrgast ein, in dem Winkel zwischen
ihrem Oberschenkel und dem auf die Sitzlehne gestützten Arm sah
Eduard das Profil eines Mannes mit grauen Bartstoppeln. Der
Mann nickte der Stewardeß zu, öffnete die Lippen zu einem
Lächeln und führte die Zigarette ruhig zum Mund. Mit lauterer
Stimme wiederholte die Stewardeß die Sicherheitsvorschrift,
schnurrte sie dann auf Englisch und Französisch herunter.

Nochmaliges Nicken und Lächeln, und wieder sog der Ange-
sprochene an seiner Zigarette wie jemand, der guten Willens ist,
aber weder Worte noch Zeichen versteht. Inzwischen hatten sich
die Köpfe der Umsitzenden dem störrischen Fahrgast zugewandt,
alle schienen darauf gespannt zu sein, wie das Personal mit dem
nie erlebten Ernstfall fertig würde, einige wiederholten die Vor-
schrift mit leisem Zischen. Eduard sah, wie sich Rücken und
Oberschenkel der Stewardeß strafften, wie sich ihr Arm von der
Sitzlehne löste, der ganze Körper schien plötzlich bereit zum
Sprung; Sekunden später fuhren beide Arme der Stewardeß auf die
ruhende Hand des Fahrgastes nieder, gleich darauf erschien
zwischen gespreizten Fingern die Zigarette, deren Glutteil zwischen
den violetten Fingernägeln gefährlich aufleuchtete, als sie es in
einem weiten Bogen durch die Luft führte und in einem Aschen-
becher der gegenüberliegenden Sitzreihe zerdrückte. Der Störer
hatte keinen Widerstand geleistet, vielmehr verharrte er in seinem
Lächeln, als hätte er ein wichtiges Ziel erreicht. Später sah
Hoffmann ihn in der Ankunftshalle. Hoch aufgerichtet, das Gesicht
gegen die Ankommenden gekehrt, stand er im Strom der hinaus-
drängenden Passagiere, als würde er jemanden erwarten. Er hatte
kein Gepäckstück dabei. Im Vorbeigehen bemerkte Eduard, daß der
linke Jackenärmel des Mannes in der Jackettasche steckte.

2

Ungefähr zu der Zeit, da Eduard in die Sonne schaute, sah Henry
aus dem Zugfenster. Henry war vergnügt und ausgeschlafen. Er
hatte gerade, mit ein paar einkalkulierten Rückfällen, eine nikotin-
und alkoholfreie Woche hinter sich gebracht. Als er sich, angeregt
durch eine verblichene Reklame auf einer vorbeiflitzenden Haus-
wand, die wie eine Höhlenzeichnung aussah, eine Zigarette
ansteckte, fühlte er sich stark und unversehrbar wie je. Die ganze
Nacht hatte er mit offenen Augen auf dem Bett des 1.
Klasse–Schlafwagens gelegen und nicht entscheiden können, ob er
als menschliche Fracht oder als very important person über
deutsche Bahnschwellen rollte. Im Morgengrauen war er durch
rücksichtsloses Schlagen der Eisentüren, bellende Stimmen und den
Gleichschritt schwerer Stiefel im Gang aus dem Halbschlaf geweckt
worden. Jemand hatte die Abteiltür aufgerissen und, ohne zu
fragen, das Oberlicht angeknipst. »Papiere, bitte!« Henry haßte
diesen Schritt, diese Art zu fragen, die jedes Frage- in ein

Ausrufezeichen verwandelte, überhaupt alle Zeichen, die ihn daran
erinnerten, daß er im Land der Mörder seiner Verwandten lebte.
Aber er hatte sich in diesem Land mit einem sorgfältig dosierten
Widerwillen eingerichtet und gelernt, sich das schlechte Gewissen,
das die Söhne der Mörder den Söhnen der Opfer entgegenbrachten,
zunutze zu machen. Ob der Beamte schon mal gehört habe, daß
man einen schlafenden Menschen nicht anbrüllt, dies ungefähr
hatte Henry sagen wollen. Stattdessen sagte er dies: »Den Juden-
stern finde ich nicht, aber vielleicht genügt mein Ausweis vorläufig!«

Mit gespielter Verwirrung durchsuchte er dann die Taschen
seines italienischen Leinenanzugs, murmelte etwas von seiner
strafwürdigen Vergeßlichkeit und kramte seinen Paß schließlich
unter einem Wust von Büchern, seidenen Hemden, schmutziger
Unterwäsche und Medikamenten aus seiner Reisetasche hervor. Ein
Ruck ging durch den Körper des wortführenden Beamten, er schien
Mühe zu haben, nicht die Hacken zusammenzuschlagen. Nur noch
der Form halber studierte er das Dokument, verglich Henrys Ohr
viel zu kurz mit dem Foto in dessen Paß, füllte dann einen Schein
aus, den er Henry mitsamt dem Paß zurückreichte.

»Entschuldigen Sie die Störung, gute Weiterreise!« Dies war ein
Volk von Befehlsempfängern: wenn es eines Ausnahmestatus be-
durfte, um wie ein normaler Mensch behandelt zu werden, so
mußte man diesen Status in Anspruch nehmen. Erst als sich die
Beamten mit einem zackigem Gruß verabschiedeten, bemerkte
Henry, daß unter der Mütze des zweiten, schweigsamen Beamten
lange, frisch geföhnte Haare hervorquollen. Henry zog die Abteiltür
wieder auf und streckte seine Hand in den Gang. »Kann ich Sie
sprechen, nur einen Moment? Ich wollte Ihnen etwas Wichtiges
sagen, ja, Sie meine ich!« Seine Bemerkung erzeugte eine kurze Irritation des Gleichschritts, eine Rhythmusstörung bei den kleineren
Stiefeln, aber Henry deutete sie als Versprechen.

Kurz darauf war Henry unter dem sanften Beben des wieder
anfahrenden Zuges eingeschlafen. Dabei half ihm die Vorstellung,
daß die uniformierte Blondine ihn an der Hand auf die Toilette
zog, dort vor ihm niederkniete und in seinem Schoß nach dem
Identitätszeichen suchte, das er im Abteil nicht vorgezeigt hatte.

Am Morgen war er durch die Rufe eines ambulanten Kellners
erwacht, der seinen Bufettwagen durch den Gang schob. Durch das
staubverkrustete Fenster sah er Häuserfassaden, wie von Geister-
händen bewegt, nah an die Gleise geschoben, dann wieder weit

zurück in die flache Landschaft gesetzt. In die blasigen Fassaden waren Industrieprodukte eingezeichnet, deren Namen längst verschollen waren. Die Vorhänge hinter den Fenstern der gleisnahen Häuser waren zugezogen, als schützten sie gegen den Lärm. In mäßigem Tempo und ohne anzuhalten rollte der Zug durch einen rotgeziegelten Zwischenbahnhof, dessen Baustil den umgebenden Villen nachempfunden war und frisch renoviert: dieser Bahnhof hatte den Deutschen zu Lebzeiten von Henrys Vater als Rampe für den endgültigen Abtransport der ansässigen Juden gedient.

Der Bahnsteig war nur spärlich mit Einheimischen besetzt, die kaum zu einer Geste des Willkommens fähig schienen. In keinem Bahnhof der Welt, dachte Henry, stehen so wenige freudig erregte Wartende auf dem Bahnsteig wie in der Mauerstadt. Die Abholer, die in Sandalen und kurzen Hosen herumstanden, erzeugten immerhin einen Anschein von Bewegung, indem sie sich mit mitgebrachten Handtüchern und Servietten den Schweiß von der Stirn wischten. In der Tiefe der Halle fiel eine kopfstarke Gruppe auf, die durch eine heftig winkende Frauenhand zu Henrys Fenster dirigiert wurde. Zuerst trabte die ganze Gruppe dem einfahrenden Zug entgegen, machte dann, da der Waggon erst im Rücken der Truppe zum Stehen kam, wieder kehrt. Nun löste sich eine Frauengestalt, in durchsichtiges Weiß gekleidet, aus der Großgruppe heraus und trippelte, so schnell es die roten, hochhackigen Schuhe erlaubten, auf den aussteigenden Henry zu. Henry fühlte sich mit einer Heftigkeit umarmt, als hätte er ein Zugunglück überlebt, und fühlte die Küsse einer zahllosen Verwandschaft auf seinen Wangen. Der weißhaarige Russe, den er nun für seinen Schwiegervater halten mußte, drängte seinen Wanst gegen Henrys Brustbein. Als Henry ihn breitbeinig und mit dampfenden Waden dastehen sah, fühlte er sich von einem Schwimmmeister in den Griff genommen, der ihn vor jeder Gefahr, aber nicht vor der bevorstehenden Hochzeit retten würde. Die Mutter drückte Henrys Kopf zwischen zwei so umfängliche Brüste, daß Henry bei dem Versuch, die Umarmung zu erwidern, mit Not ihre Achseln erreichte. Erst als sie von ihm abließ, entdeckte er an ihren Fingern eine hochkarätige Sammlung von Edelsteinen, die er wie einen Schlagring im Genick gespürt hatte. Die minderjährigen Geschwister hatte Henry im Verdacht, daß sie in jede Tasse Kakao zehn Eßlöffel Zucker schaufelten, und Henry beschloß, sie vorläufig nicht zu zählen.

Wie in aller Welt hatte seine Braut es vermocht, sich im Kreis der
übergewichtigen Verwandtschaft so elfenhaft zart zu erhalten?
Reumütig erinnerte Henry sich des Rats seiner Mutter: den ersten
Blick auf die Schwiegermutter, nicht auf die Geliebte werfen. Aber
nun war es zu spät. Für einen Augenblick klang Henry die
Bemerkung eines Freundes im Ohr, die ihm jetzt wie ein Ver-
sprechen erschien: er werde den Freund, hatte Eduard gesagt,
sowohl durch die Heirat wie durch die unvermeidliche Scheidung
begleiten. Henry liebte Ratschläge und er holte sie von so vielen
Seiten ein, daß sie sich unweigerlich gegenseitig aufhoben. In der
Stauzone, in der alle Ratschläge sich gegenseitig blockierten, traf
Henry dann seine Entscheidung.

3

Am gleichen Tag näherte sich aus der entgegengesetzten Richtung
Malin dem Bahnhof der westlichen Teilstadt. Gemessen an den
Anreisen von Eduard und Henry hatte die Strecke, die Malin mit
der Stadtbahn zurücklegte, kaum die Länge einer Kaffeefahrt; sie
maß etwa zehn Kilometer. Falls es jedoch ein Maß für Malins
Wahrnehmung dieser Entfernung gab, so wäre jeder Kilometer-
zähler überfordert gewesen. Ohne die Mitreisenden anzusehen,
wußte Malin, daß sie die einzige Passagierin im Zug war, die
keinen gültigen Ausweis in der Tasche hatte; der ihre war
unmittelbar vor dem Einsteigen mit dem Vermerk »Entlassung aus
der Staatsbürgerschaft« gestempelt worden. Ohne Neugier wartete
Malin auf den Augenblick, den sie sich tausendmal vorgestellt
hatte. Wenn die Brandmauern mit den zugemauerten Türen und
Fenstern auseinandertraten, würde sie die Vorderseite jenes ver-
haßten Gebäudemassivs mit dem verwitterten Reichsadler er-
blicken, das sie bisher nur von hinten gesehen hatte. In einer
Zeitspanne, die durch das Schlagen der Räder über ein Dutzend
schlecht gefügter Gleisstücke gemessen wurde, würde sie in eine
Biosphäre eintauchen, in der andere Druckverhältnisse herrschten
und die Reflexe der Menschen, die unwillkürlichen Gesten des
Anblickens und Grüßens, anderen Gesetzen gehorchten. Es störte
Malin, daß nichts außer dem schmächtigen Band aus Beton, das
den Zug eine zeitlang begleitete, ihre Ankunft in der neuen Welt
beglaubigte. Vergeblich suchte sie nach Zeichen einer anderen
Vegetation; daß dort draußen die gleichen Krüppelkastanien und
Essigbäumchen wuchsen wie in der alten Welt, erschien ihr als

Tarnung. Das Laub an den Bäumen änderte nicht seine Farbe, die Häuser, die gedächtnislos neuen wie die aufpolierten, waren ein bißchen besser gehalten, aber sprachen von keiner neuen Idee, das Licht draußen wurde nicht heller, die Luft im Waggon weder leichter noch schwerer. Nur der entgegenkommende Schnellzug, der Richtung Warschau fuhr, erzeugte sekundenlang einen wohltuenden Druck auf den Ohren. Wenn die Mitreisenden wenigstens ihren Federschmuck aus dem Koffer geholt und Malin mit rituellen, unverständlichen Gesängen umtanzt hätten, sie wäre erleichtert gewesen. Das Schlimmste war, daß Malin jedes Wort verstand.

»Da wird Pappi sich aber freuen.«

»Wir sind zu spät, solange wartet der nicht.«

»Hauptsache, wir kommen an.«

Es waren eindeutig Menschenlaute, gesprochen von extraterrestrischen Wesen, die ihre Herkunft mühsam, unter einer künstlichen Haut und einem perfekt nachgebildeten Gestrüpp aus Knochen und Sehnen verbargen.

Achtundvierzig Stunden zuvor hatte Malin überraschend die Genehmigung für die beantragte »Ausreise« erhalten, mit dem Bescheid, daß die Reise unverzüglich anzutreten sei. Auf die Fristsetzung und den amtlichen Ausdruck »Entlassung« verschwendete Malin keine Empörung. Es war ihr bekannt, daß der Staat den Wunsch eines Bürgers nach einer Ausreise als eine persönliche Kränkung, juristisch gesprochen, als »böswilliges Verlassen« empfand; offenbar konnte der Staat dem Wunsch nach Trennung nur stattgeben, indem er die Ausreise als Hinauswurf inszenierte. Dieses Machogehabe, das Malin von einigen ihrer Liebhaber kannte, hatte sie in diesem Fall ausnahmsweise gerührt. Es kam, ihres Wissens, nicht oft vor, daß ein Staat sich wie ein enttäuschter Liebhaber aufführte; aber um nichts geringeres als um eine gescheiterte Liebe ging es wohl.

In den gewährten achtundvierzig Stunden war wenig Zeit für Abschiede geblieben. Wahllos verschenkte Malin Möbel, Bücher, Schallplatten, ererbtes Meißner Geschirr an zufällig Vorbeikommende und an Nachbarn. Bei denen konnte sie immerhin sicher sein, daß sie ihre Tellerchen und Dampfbügeleisen loswurde, ohne sie mit Entschuldigungen und Rückkehrabsichten bekleben zu müssen. Die eifersüchtige Aufmerksamkeit, mit der der Staat ihren Abgang beobachtete, erkannte sie auch in den Augen und Stimmen ihrer Verwandten und Freunde. Es war schwer zu entscheiden, auf welche Energie diese unerbetene Aufmerksamkeit gegründet war:

auf den Wunsch zum Dableiben oder zum Abhauen, jedenfalls handelte es sich um eine ziemlich große Energie. Malin hatte es deswegen vorgezogen, möglichst ungesehen zu verschwinden. Bei ihren Abschiedsbesuchen und bei letzten Telefongesprächen benahm sie sich wie eine Gehetzte, die keine Zeit für Erklärungen hat.

»Ja, am Dienstag in den Westen, und auf Wiedersehen, bis bald oder dort.«

Ob als Verräterin oder heimlich Beneidete, Malin glaubte den Bleistift zu hören, mit dem sie aus den Adreßbüchern gestrichen wurde. Die berühmte Frage, welche zehn Bücher man mitnehmen würde, wenn man das restliche Leben auf einer unbewohnten Insel zu verbringen hätte, beantwortete Malin, indem sie alles zurückließ. Sie packte eine einzige Tüte, in der sie nur ein paar Briefe, Fotos und Notizen verstaute; dies tat sie nicht etwa, weil sie den Kram mitnehmen, sondern weil sie ihn nicht zurücklassen wollte. Sie verließ die halbe Stadt, in der sie geboren war, mit derselben Plastiktüte in der Hand, mit der die Extraterrestrischen aus dem Intershop heimkehrten: jene hatten eine um acht Mark verbilligte Stange Westzigaretten in der Hand, Malin die schlecht sortierten Reste ihres 26-jährigen Lebens. Als der Zug sein Tempo verlangsamte, sah Malin hinter Gitterstäben, die wie eine endlose Reihe von Ausrufezeichen vorbeiflitzten, die Hörner gewaltiger Nasentiere, gleich darauf einen Elefanten, dessen Kopf mit entsetzlicher Regelmäßigkeit hin und hertickte, als müsse er das Unendlichkeitszeichen in die Luft schreiben. Daß die Stadt dem Ankommenden zuerst und gratis ein paar Großtiere vorführte, nahm Malin als Geständnis. Es war gleich, ob man sich vor oder hinter den Gitterstäben aufhielt. Dies war ein Zoo, den sich ein oder zwei entfernte Direktoren zum Ergötzen der übrigen Menschheit hielten. Malin selbst rechnete sich zu den Nachttieren, die nur bei völliger Dunkelheit zum Leben erwachen. Im übrigen hatte sie gegen die Rolle des seltenen Exemplars nichts einzuwenden, vorausgesetzt, ein hoher Eintrittspreis wurde gezahlt.

2

Peter Schneider: A Biographical Sketch

COLIN RIORDAN

Peter Schneider first came to prominence by publicly rejecting the world of his parents' generation during the student revolt of 1967–9. Yet there is little in his own origins to suggest a future political activist. His mother came from a conservative family with a clerical tradition, although, according to Schneider's account, she was uneasy with the reactionary views which prevailed in her own family home.[1] His father, born in 1911, began a musical career as a church organist and choirmaster. He became a conductor, and later enjoyed some success as a composer. Although he once conducted a youth choir at an NSDAP rally in Nürnberg, he was not a party member and, as Schneider puts it: 'Er hat nie ein Gewehr in der Hand gehabt'.[2] He joined the army as a signaller and was later taken prisoner in France. In 1940 Peter Schneider was born as the third child. His younger brother Michael (who has become prominent in Germany as a writer and critic himself) was born in 1943. Towards the end of the war his mother took the four children (three boys and a girl) to her father's house in Grainau, near Garmisch-Partenkirchen. In 1948 Schneider's mother died; his father subsequently remarried, and was appointed to a post as conductor at the *Stadttheater* in Freiburg in 1950.

In Freiburg the young Schneider attended the Berthold-Gymnasium. Despite an early ambition to follow his father's musical career and become a concert violinist, it became apparent that his talent would not suffice. He readjusted his ambitions, and began writing from the age of eleven or twelve onwards. Theatre was his early passion, resulting in a number of dramatizations of Grimms' fairy tales. Contemporary theatre which made an early impression included Borchert's *Draußen vor der Tür* and Ingeborg Bachmann's radio play *Der gute Gott von Manhattan*. Later, it was dramatists such as Sartre, Camus, Ionesco, Beckett and Brecht who set an example for the aspiring playwright. Other intellectual interests were of two main types: tales of the uncanny on the one hand, and philosophy on the other; not only E. T. A. Hoffmann and Edgar Allen Poe, but also Spinoza. As one might expect, popular culture of the 1950s was an important part of his adolescence, although James Dean, Elvis Presley and Fats Domino contrasted starkly with the high culture of the Schneiders' musical home. The young man's traditional, humanist schooling concluded with the *Abitur* in 1959. He studied German, history and philosophy for two semesters at Freiburg, then spent two semesters in Munich. After a further semester in Freiburg, Schneider moved to Berlin in the spring of 1962, making the city his permanent home.

In order to achieve some financial independence from his parents (three of whose children were students at the same time), Schneider began working as a radio journalist for the *Südwestfunk*. In Freiburg, then later in Munich and Berlin, he worked on radio essays, features and criticisms. At the same time, he wrote substantial plays, which he has described as 'unverkäuflich, unglaublich ehrgeizige, riesige Projekte, immer so Hundertseitenstücke'.[3] By 1964 he was regularly publishing literary criticism and essays both in newspapers (particularly in *Die Zeit*, where Dieter E. Zimmer was a mentor) and in literary and cultural magazines such as *Neue Rundschau, Sprache im technischen Zeitalter* and *Neue Deutsche Hefte*.[4] Having embarked on a successful journalistic career, Schneider effectively gave up his studies, and was not to rematriculate until after the end of the student movement. He regarded journalism as a means of making a living: his real ambition was to be a writer, and, indeed, to become famous as quickly as possible. He had attracted enough attention to become the recipient of a grant from the *Literarisches Colloquium*, which provided for a five-month stay at a villa on the Wannsee, with the benefit of advice from established writers such as Heinar Kipphardt and Peter Rühmkorf.[5] But it became clear to Schneider that this literary retreat isolated the beneficiaries from the practicalities of everyday experience. In particular, the Federal Republic was approaching its first serious economic and political crisis, soon to be followed by social upheaval.

By 1965 the government of Ludwig Erhard was becoming unsustainable as the Chancellor himself suffered a dramatic loss of personal popularity. For the first time since the establishment of the Federal Republic, the SPD seemed to have some chance of toppling the CDU-CSU/FDP coalition. Not yet the political radical he was shortly to become, Schneider turned his writing talent to the advantage of the main opposition party as the economic crisis deepened and an election became imminent. He was invited by the publisher Klaus Wagenbach to help write speeches for the SPD campaign. He would regularly collect topics from election headquarters and compose stirring addresses, none of which, it seems, were ever used.[6] Nevertheless, he was in some exalted (and some notorious) company: his co-workers included Günter Grass, Peter Härtling, Hans-Christoph Buch, F. C. Delius, Gudrun Ensslin, Hubert Fichte, Günter Herburger and Bernward Vesper. But the result of the election was a disappointment. Many on the Left saw the decision of Willy Brandt to co-operate with the CDU-CSU in government as a betrayal of what they had fought for, especially since it included conniving at the introduction of the *Notstandsgesetze*. As the 'Außerparlamentarische Opposition' gathered momentum in the wake of the coalition of 26 November 1966, Schneider left for a six-month stay in England. Put off by the cold, damp and squalid conditions of life on a limited income in the England of the mid-1960s, Schneider returned to Berlin in 1967 with a zest for new projects. Determined to make something of his theatrical ambitions, he launched an effort to interest producers in West Germany in his idea of a dramatic secular mass: 'Die deutschen Alpträume und Wunschgebirge, die sich täglich im Straßenverkehr und in der *Bildzeitung* darstellten, sollten szenisch gebeichtet werden und keine Absolution erhalten' (*AP*, 225). To his surprise, Schneider quickly received an offer to present his ideas at the playhouse in Stuttgart.

Almost immediately, the opportunity became a dilemma. Rudi Dutschke and Hans Magnus Enzensberger persuaded him to organize a tribunal to expose the wrongdoings of the *Springer-Verlag*, publisher of the *Bildzeitung*. His decision to engage in political activism in this way simultaneously represented a rejection of his former ambition to become a playwright, and entailed a temporary suspension of all aesthetic activity. While the 'Springer-Tribunal' project was less successful than had been hoped, Schneider nevertheless came to prominence as a speaker and as a writer of political pamphlets. 'Wir haben Fehler gemacht', a speech given at a sit-in in the Audimax of the Free University of Berlin in April 1967, captured the mood of the time and thrust him into the limelight (see *AN*, 7–14). An essay entitled 'Die Phantasie im Spätkapitalismus und die Kulturrevolution',[7] which he published in Hans Magnus Enzensberger's *Kursbuch* in 1969, remains one of the key texts to articulate the world-view of the left-wing intellectuals who set the tone in the student movement. Ironically, it was during this period of anti-establishment protest that Schneider's achievements as an essayist were first given official public recognition. On 18 March 1969, Klaus Schütz, mayor of Berlin, presented Peter Schneider with the 'Literaturpreis Junge Generation', which amounted to the considerable sum of DM 5,000. Like Wolf Biermann, who received the senior prize in the literary category of the 'Berliner Kunstpreise', Schneider announced his decision to give the prize money to the APO. Alone among the ten prize-winners, however, Schneider used the occasion to demonstrate against the Vietnam war. The protest quickly turned violent as his supporters clashed with security personnel, and Schneider achieved notoriety as a supposed dangerous radical.

While Schneider was a notable figure in the student movement, and was close to Rudi Dutschke, it was not primarily for his political activity during this period that he eventually became widely known. His first publication in book form, *Ansprachen. Reden, Notizen, Gedichte*, appeared in 1970. A slim volume consisting of two speeches given during the course of the student movement, along with a number of anti-capitalist and anti-establishment polemics and poems, *Ansprachen* remains a valuable document which received generally favourable reviews without making a lasting impression. According to the publisher Klaus Wagenbach (himself a prominent supporter of the APO), Schneider had to be subjected to considerable persuasion before agreeing to publish the manuscripts. Part of the explanation may be that, as early as 1968, Schneider was experiencing doubts about the aims and ideals of the student movement and the social revolution he publicly advocated. Beset by a personal crisis arising from a collapsed relationship, he travelled to Italy in order to clear his thoughts. Two weeks of this stay were spent in trying to help Rudi Dutschke in his rehabilitation following the brain damage received after being shot in the head in an assassination attempt on 11 April 1968. It was here that Schneider wrote 'Die Phantasie im Spätkapitalismus und die Kulturrevolution' (see *AP*, 230). Yet the apparent objectivity of that essay belies the emotional turmoil which was to give rise to *Lenz* (published 1973), the work which defined his early career as a writer. The extraordinary success of this text turned Peter Schneider overnight into a literary household name. It also saddled him with the reputation of a promising young author expected to achieve greater things, an expectation which has coloured the critical reception of his work ever since. *Lenz* remains the iconic text of the student movement, even though it was only one of many to appear in the course of the 1970s. Tellingly, the story is less about the movement itself than about the hero's disillusionment with it.

But before the success of *Lenz*, Schneider had been forced by the failure of the student movement to undertake a radical reappraisal of his prospects. Having previously suspended his career as a writer, and the APO having patently failed to bring about the hoped-for revolution, Schneider opted to swallow his pride and pursue a secure profession as a teacher whilst working on the novella which was destined to make his career. He returned to his studies and completed the 'Erstes Staatsexamen' in 1972, applying as normal for the two years' teaching practice necessary for the full qualification. Ironically, this decision provided the material for his next work, for in 1973 Schneider fell victim to the so-called 'Radikalenerlaß' introduced by Willy Brandt's government on 28 January 1972. Prevented from even setting foot in schools, let alone teaching in them, Schneider used his experience as material for a number of essays,[8] and for a hastily assembled play (written in two weeks at the end of 1974) which was performed at the Kammertheater in Stuttgart on 9 January 1975. Entitled *Geschäftszeichen IAa5*, and directed by Schneider in tandem with Thomas Kirchner, the performance consisted of 'eine Collage von "alten und neuen Szenen zum Thema Radikale"'.[9] The typical Schneider mixture of historical and literary material and allusions (Schiller, Brecht, Ossietzky, Galileo) with topical instances of radical protest (including Wolf Biermann) was positively though not widely received. More famously, Schneider published his experience in lightly fictionalized form as *. . . schon bist du ein Verfassungsfeind. Das unerwartete Anschwellen der Personalakte des Lehrers Kleff* (1975). In 1976, after a judicial review, the decision of the 'Berliner Schulsenat' to exclude Schneider was revoked, and the senate was compelled to offer him a place as a *Referendar*. By this point, the high sales figures of

Lenz and the more moderate success of . . . *schon bist du ein Verfassungsfeind* allowed him to reject the offer.

Schneider continued to publish essays and reviews throughout the 1970s, the only gap in this activity appearing between 1971 and 1973. Most of this work was collected and reprinted in *Atempause. Versuch, meine Gedanken über Literatur und Kunst zu ordnen* (1977). It is fair to say that this collection, despite mixed reviews, established Schneider's reputation as an essayist after the modest impact of *Ansprachen*, a reputation which was quickly to outstrip his renown as a writer of fiction. At the same time, the volume exemplifies the evolution in Schneider's views during the 1970s. His seminal essay 'Die Phantasie im Spätkapitalismus und die Kulturrevolution' (1968) is reprinted alongside the autobiographical piece 'Die Beseitigung der ersten Klarheit'. It is clear that the strongly ideological, programmatic approach of the earlier essay has, by 1977, been replaced by a much more individual perspective. Perhaps it would be truer to say that the individual perspective has resurfaced, for in the context of Schneider's political development, the Maoist period has to be seen as a temporary phenomenon. This is not to say that Schneider became unpolitical or apolitical, merely that the approach to political problems undergoes a radical reassessment. The collection of stories published under the title *Die Wette* in 1978 confirms this view. In these stories Schneider attempts to distil the dynamics of political power, in order to show how their origins lie in struggles between individuals. In particular, the use of fear as a political weapon is explored in detail. Schneider's critical view of the ascendancy of feminism on the Left becomes apparent,[10] and the supposed 'neue Innerlichkeit' of 1970s German literature transpires, in this case, to be at least as political as the overt arguments of . . . *schon bist du ein Verfassungsfeind*. 'Der große und der kleine Bruder', the penultimate story in the collection, provides a fascinating insight into the strained relationship between Peter Schneider and his younger brother Michael. Indeed, this story marked a stage in a public disputation which may have begun as early as 1974 and continued at least until 1992.[11]

The next project was more overtly topical. The year 1977 had been one in which left-wing terrorism reached its height, as the industrialist Hanns Martin Schleyer was kidnapped and murdered, and the hostage crisis in Mogadishu took place. Andreas Baader, Gudrun Ensslin and Jan Carl Raspe died in controversial circumstances in Stammheim prison. In 1979 Rudi Dutschke died as a result of a right-wing attack eleven years earlier. By coincidence, in the same year Schneider published his screenplay for Reinhard Hauff's film *Messer im Kopf*, which had been premiered in 1978. The published text 'verhält sich zum Film wie ein Bühnentext zur Inszenierung'.[12] Perhaps surprisingly, considering his closeness to people who later became terrorists, this work is Schneider's only fictional approach to the question of violence and politics.[13] The screenplay concerns the road to recovery of Hoffmann, a biochemist, who has been shot in the head by a policeman. Rudi Dutschke is the obvious model for the brain-damaged patient. As with *Lenz*, the main protagonist is indirectly a victim of the political idealism of others. And, as in the case of Lenz, it is the personal (in the case of Hoffmann, physical) consequences of political action which are the central object of interest. The conflict between citizens and state remains on the periphery. Hauff's film was successful both critically and at the box-office, and won a number of prizes.

In 1980 Schneider travelled through five South American countries on a reading tour organized by the Goethe Institute. The experience clearly made a lasting impression which can be detected in several of the author's works since. The immediate result was the title essay of the collection *Die Botschaft des Pferdekopfs und andere Essais aus einem friedlichen Jahrzehnt*, which was published in October 1981. 'Die Botschaft des Pferdekopfs', a mixture of travel writing, cultural analysis and mild capitalist critique, is accompanied by a collection of essays written and published elsewhere during the 1970s. They include pieces on the student movement and associated political critique, documents prepared for Schneider's defence against the charge of being a 'Verfassungsfeind', articles on the treatment of the Baader-Meinhof terrorists, and an essay on male reaction to the feminist movement.

Schneider's next big success after *Lenz* was to come the following year. *Der Mauerspringer* (1982) was the first West German literary text (although the story is in many ways a collection of essays) to take the division of Germany as its subject since Uwe Johnson's *Zwei Ansichten* in 1965. The success of *Der Mauerspringer* demonstrated one extraordinary talent which Schneider seems to possess: the ability to identify and articulate a problem or question which has a previously unsuspected resonance with the reading public, or indeed with the collective consciousness of the nation.

While the German question was to dominate serious public debate in the Federal Republic as the 1980s progressed, nobody encapsulated the emotive and epistemological problem as neatly and clearly as Schneider: 'Die Mauer im Kopf einzureißen wird länger dauern, als irgendein Abrißunternehmen für die sichtbare Mauer braucht' (*MS*, 102). These words were repeated endlessly in the overwhelmingly positive reviews of *Der Mauerspringer*, and are quoted almost as often in academic studies of the work. *Der Mauerspringer* not only enhanced Schneider's reputation, but it supplied him with a kind of prophetic authority on the subject of division and unification which was later to stand him in good stead. In the same year Schneider renewed his partnership with Reinhard Hauff to make the story into a film with the title *Der Mann auf der Mauer*.

In 1983 Schneider began writing *Paarungen*, a novel which was not to appear for a further nine years. He continued producing essays at regular intervals, including a critical view of the burgeoning peace movement with special reference to the approach of fundamentalist Greens, entitled 'Keine Lust aufs grüne Paradies' (1983). Green issues also formed part of his next project. The journey through South America had furnished material for a drama, which Schneider supplemented by some years of research. The result was to be his first serious play. *Totoloque. Das Geiseldrama von Mexiko-Tenochtitlán* was first performed as a radio play on 1 June 1985, and opened at the Munich *Residenztheater* on 4 July 1985 under the direction of Wilfried Minks. The playwright had hoped to explore dramatically the problems of cultural conflict which had emerged in the essay 'Die Botschaft des Pferdekopfs'. The disputes and power struggles between the conqueror Cortés and his captive Moctezuma were to provide the dramatic focus whilst a chorus commented on the action, drawing contrasts and parallels with modern environmental awareness. However, the action moved slowly, the atmosphere was flat. Audience reaction was negative, the reviews disastrous. Schneider admits that his first serious drama was a failure.[14] But the disaster of *Totoloque* was not the only major event of 1985 for Schneider. The year was also marked by a four-week journey through China with Hans-Christoph Buch, Helga Novak, Heinz Ludwig Arnold and Wolfgang Kubin, which Schneider documented in a travel essay published in *Die Zeit*. And in May 1985 *Ratte – tot . . . Ein Briefwechsel* was published.

This volume was the result of a protracted correspondence with the convicted, imprisoned terrorist Peter-Jürgen Boock. Schneider introduces the correspondence, and where necessary, provides explanatory linking notes, in particular concerning the death of his half-brother Nicolas from cancer in 1983. The efforts to find a cure for Nicolas by visiting a specialist in Paris are later echoed in the illness of André in *Paarungen*. The volume was reasonably successful, and was reprinted in October. It is clear from the correspondence that a powerful bond of trust and affection had formed between the convicted terrorist and the writer. That bond was severely shaken when, several years later, Boock finally admitted that he had in fact committed the murder of which he had always assured the world – and his friend Schneider – that he was innocent. Meanwhile, Schneider was to turn his attention to entirely different matters.

In June 1985 Rolf Mengele, son of the Auschwitz doctor Josef Mengele, revealed in a series of articles in *Bunte Illustrierte* that his father had died in Brazil six years before. Mengele was still being sought as one of the world's most wanted criminals; the news of his whereabouts and death was sensational. Peter Schneider was struck by the coincidence that Rolf Mengele had grown up in Freiburg, had probably been to the same school, and was a leftish liberal of roughly the same generation. The *Bunte* articles explained how in 1977 Rolf Mengele had visited Brazil to see the father he had never known. Drawing on his own experience of visiting Brazil in 1980, Schneider fictionalized this aspect of the story in the form of the 'Erzählung' *Vati*, which was published in 1987. A few days before the volume went on sale, however, it – and the author – were subjected to a scathing attack in the columns of *Der Spiegel*. Fundamentally, the complaint was that Schneider had plagiarized from the *Bunte* articles. The result was a literary scandal with legal implications. Columnists took sides and Schneider went on television to debate the issue publicly. Again Schneider had found a topical issue which called forth vigorous reaction amongst public commentators, although the reaction was rather less welcome on this occasion. The charge of plagiarism was not in general accepted, but the writer had to endure some harsh criticism of his literary ability, his sensitivity to the past and his judgement. A year later, in an essay entitled 'Vom richtigen Umgang mit dem Bösen', which concludes the collection *Deutsche Ängste*, Schneider mounted an able defence of both his approach to the legacy of Auschwitz and of his judgement, though he wisely left the question of literary quality to others to decide.[15]

In March and April 1989, Schneider wrote an essay entitled 'Was wäre, wenn die Mauer fällt'. Translated, this appeared in the *New York Times Magazine* of 25 June 1989. The author had taken as a starting-point for his speculations Ronald Reagan's rhetorical appeal in a speech held in Berlin in 1987: 'Mr Gorbachev, tear down this wall!' On 9 November 1989, Schneider was in America as a writer in residence when he heard that the border between East and West had indeed been opened. Coincidence it may be, but Schneider's apparent prescience on this occasion was startling. The essay was to form part of an extraordinarily successful collection entitled *Extreme Mittellage. Eine Reise durch das deutsche Nationalgefühl*, published in September 1990. So successful was this work, indeed, that it was reissued in an expanded and revised version in 1992. Translated into English as *The German Comedy*, *Extreme Mittellage.* confirmed Schneider's position as a media expert on the social effects of division and unification. The 1990s marked a renaissance in Schneider's reputation as he returned to more familiar themes after the critical disasters of *Totoloque* and *Vati*. In 1992 he published *Paarungen*, his first novel. Critically, the novel had something of a mixed reception, although reviews were in the main positive. Selling over 50,000 copies in hardback alone, the novel was extremely well received by the reading public. The blend of humour with story-telling and essayistic analysis, coupled with a subject matter set in pre-unification West Germany, reached a level of popular appeal rare in a literary novel in German. The growth in the writer's stature is evident from the expensively produced hardback which contains his most recent publication at the time of writing, *Vom Ende der Gewißheit* (1994). The pieces in this collection are a testament to Schneider's reputation as an essayist.

While Schneider is unquestionably a talented and important writer, it is still too early to come to any firm conclusion about his aesthetic standing in the context of post-1968 German literature. What is beyond question is his ability to identify the issue of the moment before many other commentators, and to articulate the problem in a way which catches the imagination of readers. His drift to the right from his earlier fiery Maoism has dismayed many on the Left. In particular, his support for changes to the constitutional provisions governing political asylum in the early 1990s gave rise to charges that the former revolutionary had moved into the camp of Helmut Kohl. Though clearly unfounded, the accusation itself is indicative of the passions which this writer is repeatedly capable of provoking, and which in themselves make his work continually valuable.

Notes

[1] From an interview with Colin Riordan and Rhys W. Williams held in December 1993, an edited version of which appears in Chapter 3 of this volume.

[2] See Peter Schneider, *Vati*, edited by Colin Riordan (Manchester, Manchester University Press, 1993), 2.

[3] Interview with Colin Riordan and Rhys W. Williams, December 1993.

[4] See the bibliography in this volume for a full list.

[5] See the autobiographical essay 'Die Beseitigung der ersten Klarheit', *AP*, 207–34 for further details.

[6] Some have been published, however. See, for example, 'Sechzehn Jahre sind genug. Redeentwurf von Peter Schneider für Willy Brandt', in Klaus Roehler and Rainer Nitsche (eds.), *Das Wahlkontor deutscher Schriftsteller in Berlin 1965. Versuch einer Parteinahme* (Berlin, :TRANSIT, 1990), 92–6, and Klaus Wagenbach, Winfried Stephan and Michael Krüger (eds.), *Vaterland, Muttersprache. Deutsche Schriftsteller und ihr Staat seit 1945* (Berlin, Wagenbach, 1979), 230, 231.

[7] *Kursbuch 16* (1969), 1–37, reprinted in *AP*, 127–61.

[8] See *BP*, 146–74.

[9] Wolfgang Ignée, 'Ein Stück in Anführungsstrichen. Gespräch mit Peter Schneider über das Radikalenerlaß-Szenarium im Kammertheater', *Stuttgarter Zeitung*, 9 January 1975. The play was later published under the title 'Alte und neue Szenen zum Thema "Radikale"', in *Theaterstücke zum Radikalenerlaß. Texte, Bilder und Dokumente* (Offenbach, Verlag 2000, 1978), 15–65.

[10] See pp. 27–8 of the interview with Peter Schneider in this volume for more information on this point.

[11] See p. 80 of R. M. Gillett's article and pp. 98–9 of my article in this volume for fuller treatments of this fraternal quarrel.

[12] See the prefatory note to *MK*.

[13] See pp. 32–3 of the interview with Schneider in this volume.

[14] See pp. 30–2 of the interview with Schneider in this volume.

[15] For a fuller discussion of the *Vati* affair, see my edition (note 2 above), and Peter Morgan, 'The Sins of the Fathers: A Reappraisal of the Controversy about Peter Schneider's *Vati*', *German Life and Letters*, 47 (1994), 104–33.

3

Gespräch mit Peter Schneider

COLIN RIORDAN UND RHYS WILLIAMS

Zu Lenz

RW: An *Lenz* fällt auf, daß sowohl komische wie auch surrealistische Stellen dabei sind, die fast nichts mit der Politik zu tun haben.

PS: Das war die politische wie die ästhetische Operation in dem Buch, die Nebensachen zu den Hauptsachen zu erklären, das Unwichtige zum Wichtigen und das Wichtige zum Unwichtigen. Es ist ein Buch über die Nachtseite dieser Studentenbewegung, über all das, was an Träumen, Wünschen, Ängsten, auch an Ehrgeiz, Rachegefühlen im öffentlichen Diskurs nicht zugelassen wurde. Daß wir äußerst ambitionierte Leute waren, daß wir ebenso aber auch liebebedürftig waren, liebestoll, sexbesessen – diese nichtformulierte, im Diskurs ausgelassene Seite sollte zum Ausdruck kommen. Deswegen habe ich ständig solche Umwege gesucht, daß Lenz zum Beispiel auf eine Frage nicht anwortet, sondern nur auf das hört, was nicht gesagt wird. Es gibt die Szene mit dem Kritiker, wo Lenz dessen Tonfall immer nur verstärkt und sagt: So, jetzt müssen wir diese Vase runterschmeissen oder die Bücher aus dem Regal reißen – offensichtlich ist es das, was Sie meinen. Es sind Vorschläge, dem rationalen politischen Diskurs zu entkommen. Wenn Lenz zum Beispiel fragt: »Haben Sie nie bemerkt, daß die Zahl der Fenster in einem Haus mit den Stockwerken zusammengerechnet immer eine ungerade Zahl ergibt?« da behauptet er natürlich einen Quatsch. Es ging darum, die Aufmerksamkeit woanders hinzulenken, eine andere, vorrationale Logik auszuprobieren.

RW: Es gibt Motive, die man sozusagen politisch deuten kann, Kleider zum Beispiel, dauernd werden Kleider anprobiert, die nicht passen oder passen. Und Lenz kriegt neue Kleider am Ende des Buchs.

PS: Im Grunde will er doch sehen, wer er ist. Er hat das Gefühl, daß er sich überhaupt nicht findet in der Rolle, die er spielt, und daß die anderen sich auch nicht finden.

RW: Und er findet sich am Ende, indem er die Kleider von anderen trägt.

PS: Am Schluß in Trento wird er neu eingekleidet. Er findet sich, indem er sich verliert, indem er seine alten Sachen ablegt. Man hat damals behauptet, das Buch beschreibe eine Identitätssuche. Ich gestehe, ich kann das Wort inzwischen nicht mehr hören: Identität. Mir ist es unheimlich, wenn Deutsche sich auf die Suche nach ihrer Identität begeben. Eine Identität findet man auf keinen Fall dann, wenn man sie sucht. Ich denke, wir Deutsche brauchen nicht mehr Identität als wir haben; die Voraussetzung wäre ja, wir hätten gar keine. Deswegen möchte ich das Problem etwas niedriger hängen. Lenz versucht lediglich, aus einer falschen Rolle, aus einer Identität, die ihn behindert, herauszukommen. Tatsächlich ist er hinterher ein anderer, als er vorher war. Aber das heißt nicht, daß er »fertig« ist, seine »Identität gefunden« hätte. Identität ist sowieso nichts, was man finden könnte und dann in der Tasche hätte.

RW: Also »Dableiben« bedeutet Alles und Nichts?

PS: Ein fast programmatisch offenes Ende. Damals – ich war noch sehr stark unter der ideologischen Fuchtel der Studentenbewegung – hatte ich natürlich andere Schlüsse geschrieben. Daß Lenz sich jetzt ins rege politische Leben stürzt, was er dabei für neue Ansätze verfolgt! Aber das »Neue« wäre schon wieder das Alte gewesen: wieder eine Formel, wieder nur ein Begriff – wieder etwas »Wichtiges«, was dieses Buch »wichtig« gemacht hätte: »Lenz zeigt den Ausweg«! Daß er stattdessen einfach nur dableiben will, ist ein Understatement. Natürlich hat er Pläne. Aber er verrät sie nicht.

CR: *Lenz* ist eine Erzählung über den Nachklang der Studenten- bewegung, aber inwieweit ist diese Erzählung auch ein Werk der

60er Jahre mit allen zugehörigen Wahrnehmungsstörungen? Man denkt da an Handke.

PS: Die Erzählung ist im Kontext der 60er Jahre entstanden. Für mich war das Produktivste an der Bewegung – was dann so schnell verloren ging – das Gefühl, daß eine neue Wahrnehmungswelt entdeckt wird. Es gab damals ein Lied, »See me, feel me, touch me« von »The Who«. Es besang diese neue Art, den anderen sich zu nähern, sie zu berühren, sie wahrzunehmen. Es war wirklich eine Revolution der Wahrnehmungsweisen und der Verhaltensweisen. Teil dieser neuen Wahrnehmung war die Verstörung, so eine Art gestörter Wahrnehmung, man kann auch von Übersensibilität sprechen – vermutlich ein Reflex auf den entsprechenden Mangel der Nazigeneration. Was *Lenz* angeht: Für mich war dieses Buch ein Versuch, aus einer ganz manifesten persönlichen Störung, aus einem existenzbedrohenden Wahn herauszukommen. Ich befand mich in einer lebensgefährlichen Krise nach einer gescheiterten Liebesgeschichte, und die Dame, um die es in meinem privaten Leben ging, war eine Übersensible wie der Lenz. Ich habe mir diese Geschichte angeeignet, in dem ich die Wahrnehmungswelt der realen Person diesem Lenz angeschrieben habe: Befreiung, gelungene Trennung durch Aneignung dieser fremden Wahrnehmung. Und insofern ist es schon richtig, wenn man sagt, daß Literatur heilen kann. Sie ändert ja nicht das Problem, aber sie erlaubt einen neuen Zugang dazu. *Lenz* war eine Art Rettungsversuch – und er gelang. Was die literarischen Einflüsse angeht, so war ich damals beeindruckt, aber auch sehr befremdet von Peter Handke.

CR: Vor allem kommen in *Die Angst des Tormanns beim Elfmeter* ähnliche Wahrnehmungsstörungen vor.

PS: Ja, diese Prosa lebt von dem besessenen Blick auf die »Nebensachen«, die Kleinigkeiten; allerdings hat mich bei Handke das Zelebrieren dieser neuen Aufmerksamkeit und der Weltverlust immer gestört: Um mich herum ist alles ekelhaft, nur dieses kostbare Ich mit seinen kostbaren Fühlern ist wichtig. Eigentlich hat er außer seinem Kind und seiner Mutter nie jemand anderen mit Zuwendung beschreiben können. Der stärkste Einfluß für mich war tatsächlich Büchners *Lenz* – das Springende, das Zerrissene der Wahrnehmung.

Zum Feminismus

CR: Welchen Einfluß hatte der werdende Feminismus in den 70er Jahren? Ich denke vor allem an die Geschichte 'Experiment mit mehreren Männern' in *Die Wette*.

PS: Einen sehr großen. Der Protest der Frauen war für uns alle eine enorme Herausforderung. Wir glaubten ja, wir hätten den Protest gepachtet, wir, die Söhne der Nazigeneration hätten ein Copyright auf diese Form. Plötzlich sahen wir Männer uns als Objekte eines ebenso heftigen Protestes seitens der Frauen. Und wir konnten nicht behaupten, das ist alles Quatsch, »konterrevolutionär«, was die Frauen sagen. Es war offensichtlich, daß sie recht hatten. Das hat einen sehr großen Einfluß auch auf mein Schreiben gehabt – siehe zum Beispiel meine Short Stories. Allerdings habe ich mich in eine andere Richtung bewegt als viele . . . »Leidensgenossen«, oder »Tätergenossen«. Ich habe ziemlich früh das peinliche Schauspiel karikiert, das entsteht, wenn Männer sich als die besseren Feministen aufführen und sich dem Problem durch Umarmung zu entziehen versuchen . . .

CR: . . . irgendwie sich auch zu den Opfern rechnen wollen . . .

PS: . . . um auf diese Weise wieder als Opfer dazustehen, natürlich. Man war ja »Opfer einer patriarchalischen Erziehung«, man war total »verkrüppelt und verbildet«, »liebesunfähig« etc. Die Selbstverleugnung ging so weit, daß Männer sich bitter darüber beklagten, daß sie nach einer Trennung abends durch die Kneipen zogen – auf der Suche nach einer Frau. Sie haben die Welt dafür angeklagt, daß ihnen dieses lästige Schicksal widerfuhr, Mann zu sein. Der männliche Feminist, das konnte nicht die Antwort auf den Feminismus sein. Ausgerechnet in einer feministischen Zeitung fand ich die Überschrift: »Der Softie ist auch keine Lösung«. Das sollte wohl heißen: Der Feminismus zwingt zwar die Männer dazu, die eigene Rolle in Frage zu stellen, aber nicht etwa dazu, sie aufzugeben und zu leugnen. Das sagen inzwischen die klügeren Feministinnen: Männer und Frauen sind grundverschieden, und es führt zu nichts, wenn sie diese Verschiedenheit verleugnen. Was beseitigt werden muß, ist nicht die Verschiedenheit, sondern die sozialen Vorteile bzw. Nachteile, die angeblich aus dem Unterschied folgen.

CR: Man spürt manchmal in der *Wette* und auch im *Mauerspringer* nicht gerade Feindlichkeit, aber eine gewisse kritische Einstellung gegenüber einer bestimmten Art von radikalem Feminismus.

PS: Mich hat die Ideologisierung dieses richtigen Ansatzes gestört, schon dieses Buch von Alice Schwarzer *Der kleine Unterschied*. Es ist eben nicht ein kleiner Unterschied zwischen den Geschlechtern, sondern ein großer. Aber meine Erzählungen handeln auch von der tiefen Irritierung der Männer. Deren Ratlosigkeit, ja deren blinder Beifall hat die Frauen dann teilweise noch weiter in ideologische Raserei hineingetrieben, sie sogar begünstigt. Wenn gar kein Widerstand kommt, wenn das Offensichtliche nicht gesagt wird aus Angst vor der Anklage . . .

CR: Gab es denn Anklagen als Antwort auf diese Texte?

PS: Nein, das ist das Überraschende gewesen. Von den Frauen kam eher Beifall. Elfriede Jelinek zum Beispiel, die in diesem Punkt sehr heftig werden kann, fand die Erzählungen toll. Vielleicht auch weil die Männer in der *Wette* samt und sonders Schwächlinge sind, was ich heute eher kritisch sehe. Schwache Männer sind ja nicht angreifbar, sie geben alles zu, selbst das, was ihnen niemand vorwirft. Die Männer in *Die Wette* sind Männer, die es mit sich machen lassen und dabei in irgendeine verrückte Situation geraten, aus der am Ende immer die Frauen als Sieger hervorgehen.

Zu den Problemen des Erzählens

RW: Es gibt bei Ihnen einen Erzählgestus, »Erzähle!« heißt das. Er leitet immer eine neue Erzählung ein, und man findet das sehr oft bei Jurek Becker. Und ich würde ganz gerne einmal etwas über die Beziehung Peter Schneider – Jurek Becker erfahren.

PS: Ich kannte Jurek Becker natürlich schon, bevor ich ihn kennenlernte. Wir sind befreundet. Wir sehen uns nicht oft, deswegen gerne. Aber ich glaube nicht, daß wir uns gegenseitig beeinflussen, obwohl wir in der Öffentlichkeit hin und wieder zusammengerückt werden. Iris Radisch, die *Zeit*-Kritikerin, hat in ihrer Wut über das, was sie den »neuen Realismus« nennt, sogar eine Firma erfunden: »Die BeckerSchneiderWalser« – ja, in einem

Wort geschrieben, als wären wir ein Großbetrieb wie Mercedes oder VW. Aber Iris Radisch interessiert sich nicht für Bücher, für Literatur, sondern nur für Literaturprogramme. Die Tatsache, daß es bei mir immer solche Brüche gibt und die Erzählung neu einsetzt, erklärt sich daraus, daß ich mich bisher immer nur in einer Mischform wohlgefühlt habe, die mir erlaubte, meine essayistischen Neigungen oder Obsessionen in Prosa aufzulösen oder umgekehrt. *Der Mauerspringer* wird dadurch vielleicht sogar ruiniert. Er ist ja eben doch mehr ein Essay als ein erzählendes Buch.

RW: Erzählungen . . . oder Essay mit Erzählungen.

PS: Eine essayistische Erzählung. Da setzt immer jemand neu ein. Darin äußert sich natürlich auch ein Mißtrauen gegen die selbstverständliche Handhabung und Bedienung dieses Gestus: Ich erzähle euch jetzt, wie die Welt ist. Diejenigen, die da Zweifel angemeldet haben – und diese Zweifel sind ja nicht von Handke und Botho Strauß erfunden, sondern seit Anfang dieses Jahrhunderts bekannt gemacht worden, etwa durch Robert Musil – haben ja durchaus berechtigte Fragen gestellt: Können wir die Welt überhaupt noch durch Geschichten darstellen, erleben wir die Wirklichkeit überhaupt in der Gestalt einer Geschichte? Diese Fragen waren absolut notwendig. Was diejenigen, die sie gestellt haben, dann jeweils für Antworten gefunden haben, ist eine andere Sache. Übrigens muß man sich auch den Meister Musil genauer anschauen. In der Literatur genügt es nie, ein Programm zu haben. Die Umsetzung muß ästhetisch überzeugen, sie muß »glücken«. Daß ich stark von Musil beeinflußt bin, von seinem essayistischen Erzählstil, ist leicht zu erkennen. Aber das heißt nicht, daß ich seinen *Mann ohne Eigenschaften* immer für gelungen halte. Ich finde zum Beispiel, daß die essayistischen Stränge sich teilweise derart verselbständigen, daß man nicht mehr zurückfindet in die Erzählung oder nachschlagen muß, was da zuletzt erzählt worden ist. Oder das Erzählte interessiert einen gar nicht mehr nach diesem langen Exkurs. Das »richtige« Verhältnis zwischen Essay und Erzählung ist in hohem Maße ein Rhythmusproblem, es verlangt eine Balance. *Der Mauerspringer* leidet vielleicht darunter, daß es keine Figur gibt, die das Ganze zusammenhält. Dieser Erzähler hat ja kein Gesicht, oder? Die bloße Absicht, nicht mehr plan zu erzählen, genügt nicht; und für ihre glückliche Umsetzung gibt es kein Rezept. Man soll sich also keine Illusionen machen. Ich bilde

mir nicht ein, daß meine Art zu erzählen *die* neue Antwort wäre
auf unsere Wirklichkeitserfahrung, daß man nur so erzählen könne
oder dürfe. Diese ganzen »man kann nur noch« oder »man darf
nicht mehr«, oder »das ist längst überwunden«, solche Hurra-
Formeln sind einfach lächerlich, und die entsprechenden Propheten
sind Ignoranten, Angeber oder Lügner. Es ist nie etwas »endgültig
überwunden«, auch der viel bescholtene Realismus wird nie
endgültig überwunden sein. Albert Camus hat in seinen Tage-
büchern den schönen Satz dazu gesagt: »Alle Ästhetiken, soweit
Schriftsteller sie hervorgebracht haben, waren immer nur heroische
Versuche, ihre eigenen künstlerischen Grenzen als objektive Gesetze
der Kunst auszugeben.« Ein Schriftsteller kann nicht »wählen«, wie
er erzählt, er hat nicht beliebig viele Erzählhaltungen zur Auswahl.
Insofern lügen alle, die behaupten, man könne nur noch so und so
erzählen oder schreiben. Ein Schriftsteller, der behauptet, *man* kann
nicht mehr erzählen, sagt eigentlich nur, daß er, dieser bestimmte
Schriftsteller, nicht erzählen kann. Das genügt eigentlich als Aus-
sage, oder?

Zu Totoloque

CR: Wie entstand Ihr Theaterstück *Totoloque*?

PS: Auf das Thema bin ich 1980, durch eine vom Goethe-Institut
organisierte Reise durch Lateinamerika gestoßen. In Brasilien habe
ich Werner Herzog getroffen, der gerade seinen *Fitzcarraldo* drehte.
Werner hat mich auf das Buch von Bernal Díaz del Castillo
hingewiesen: *Die Entdeckung und Eroberung von Neuspanien.* Und das
habe ich dann gelesen. Ein erster Niederschlag dieser Lektüre
findet sich in dem Essay »Die Botschaft des Pferdekopfs«. Mich hat
vor allem der völlig unvorbereitete Zusammenstoß dieser beiden
Kulturen fasziniert: der christlich-kolonialistischen und der
indianischen – eine Grenzerfahrung von einer unerhörten Dimension. Grenzen haben mich seit jeher fasziniert. Ob es die Grenze
zwischen den beiden Deutschland war (wie zum Beispiel im
Mauerspringer) oder die zwischen Privatem und Politik, die in *Lenz*
dramatisiert wird. Und hier nun die Grenze zwischen der
»siegreichen« europäischen und der vernichteten Kultur der
Naturvölker. Ein anderes Buch hat mich dabei enorm beeinflußt,
das großartige Buch von Tzvetan Todorov, dem französischen, von

Hause aus bulgarischen Essayisten. Es heißt: *La Conquête de Mexique. Qui est l'Autre*, »Wer ist der Andere«. Ich wollte den bei Todorov skizzierten Zweikampf der beiden Männer in einer Art Boule-Spiel dramatisieren. Das Spiel Totoloque habe ich nicht erfunden, Cortés und Moctezuma haben es gespielt, über die Regeln ist allerdings nichts bekannt. Die ganze Idee zu diesem Stück fußt auf drei oder vier Zeilen bei Bernal Díaz del Castillo. Irgendetwas mit der Sache ist mir aber schiefgegangen. Was mit so einer Idee schiefgehen kann, habe ich bei der Inszenierung in München gesehen. Ich hatte immer die Vorstellung, das Spiel müßte in einem Spielsalon inszeniert werden, in einer Fabrikhalle zum Beispiel, die ummontiert wäre zu einer großen gambling hall, wo also Billard und an Spielautomaten gespielt wird. Und mittendrin wären dann plötzlich diese beiden Männer. Ihr Spiel dürfte nicht in einem historisch definierten Raum stattfinden. Von wegen Spielhalle; in München war ein ganz strenger sakraler Raum gebaut worden, und es herrschte von Anfang an eine Totenstimmung. Den ganzen Abend lang ist das Stück aus dieser Totenstimmung nie herausgekommen. Aber der Fehler lag nicht nur bei der Inszenierung, er findet sich im Stück selbst. Ich habe keinen Rahmen gebaut, der diesen heutigen, aktuellen Zugriff zwingend macht. Ich war zu fasziniert von den herrlichen Texten Bernardino Sahagúns, die ich dem Chor gegeben habe: Erzählungen der überlebenden Azteken. Das ist das Problem an diesem Stück, daß man von Anfang an in einen musealen Raum gestellt wird. Dabei hatte ich nie Schwierigkeiten mit der Frage, warum ein Mensch aus Berlin diese Geschichte heute erzählt. Wir könnten keine einzige Geschichte heute erzählen oder verstehen, weder aus der antiken noch aus irgendeiner anderen Welt, wenn es nicht irgendeinen Rest gäbe, der in jedem von uns überlebt. Aus der Genforschung wissen wir, daß wir alle diese Stadien noch einmal durchlaufen, vom Einzeller über den Fisch zum Säugetier. So muß es sich wohl auch mit den Epochen der Menschheitsgeschichte verhalten. Wir könnten die Gedanken der Indianer nicht verstehen, wenn wir nicht selber noch – zu 0,8 Prozent – Indianer wären.

CR: Wie wichtig war das Thema Ausbeutung der Umwelt, Ausbeutung der Welt durch die erste Welt?

PS: Der überwältigende Eindruck bei dieser Reise war, daß diese »neue Welt« vollkommen durch uns geformt und geprägt ist, was natürlich das Ergebnis einer Gewaltgeschichte ist. Warum sind wir eigentlich entsetzt, wenn der Mast einer Überlandleitung am Amazonas steht, der uns im Schwarzwald nicht mehr stört? Ich hatte plötzlich das Gefühl, ich könnte diese ganze europäische Zivilisation von unten anschauen wie eine Topfpflanze, die man aus dem Topf herausnimmt und hochhebt, um ihre Wurzeln von unten zu betrachten. Das war das Gefühl, das ich hatte, als ich diese Geschichte von Cortés und Moctezuma las, das hat mir eigentlich den Impetus gegeben. Es war ein sehr ehrgeiziges Unterfangen, ich habe sehr viel Zeit darauf verwandt. Ich recherchiere ziemlich viel, wenn ich schreibe. Ich setze mir immer vor, beim Schreiben etwas herauszufinden, was ich noch nicht weiß. Das betrifft sowohl das Schreiben selbst, wie auch den Gegenstand. In *Paarungen* war es die Genetik, und hier also der Zusammenstoß zwischen Cortés und Moctezuma – wohl einer der verrücktesten und unglaublichsten »Unfälle«, die unsere Geschichte aufzuweisen hat.

Zu *Peter-Jürgen Boock und* Ratte – tot

CR: Wie stehen Sie jetzt zu *Ratte – tot?*

PS: 1967/68 hatte ich erlebt, daß wir nicht etwa nur zu fünft, sondern zu Tausenden über die Notwendigkeit revolutionärer Gewalt diskutiert hatten. Es gab in der Studentenbewegung niemals eine generelle Absage an Gewalt. Schließlich wollte man ja eine Revolution machen. Und eine Revolution ganz ohne Gewalt, so dachten wir, kann es nicht geben. Es war also nur die Frage: Wann ist Gewalt gerechtfertigt, und welche Art der Gewalt? Die RAF ist nicht etwa in einem Geheimzirkel entstanden, in dem sich ein paar Verrückte diese entlegenen Gedanken machten. Die RAF war die extreme und realitätsblinde Reaktion auf einen Diskurs, an dem Tausende von Leuten teilgenommen haben. Ich selber war durch persönliche wie ideelle Beziehungen in großer Nähe zu dieser Sache, man hat auch versucht, mich in eine der Gruppen hineinzuziehen. Das habe ich zum Glück abgelehnt, aus, wie ich heute sagen muß, eher dürftigen Gründen. Es war eher ein Instinkt als eine klare moralische Position, der mich zurückgehalten hat. Später, als man die Folgen sah, war es viel einfacher, eine grundsätzliche Ablehnung zu begründen. Aber die Rotarmisten der ersten Stunde hatten ja auch noch nicht erlebt und erfahren, was bei ihrer Gewaltstrategie herauskommt: daß man »unschuldige« Leute umbringt, oder die »Falschen« trifft – verräterische Worte. Denn die »Richtigen«, die man auf diese Weise treffen könnte, gibt es nicht. Ich hatte immer das Gefühl einer Verantwortung, nicht weil ich persönlich zum bewaffneten Kampf aufgerufen hätte, das ist nicht der Fall gewesen. Aber ich war Teil einer Studentenbewegung, die über diese Möglichkeit diskutiert und all zuviel offen gelassen hatte. Als ich dann sah, wie schrecklich sich die Praxis der RAF entwickelte, habe ich mich gefragt, wie eine Umkehr auf diesen Irrweg aussehen könnte. Peter-Jürgen Boock war damals der Einzige in Deutschland, – aus Italien kannte ich einige Vorgänger – der die in meinen Augen einzig mögliche Haltung vorgeführt hat: dem Irrsinn absagen, sagen: daß die Strategie falsch war, »schmeißt die Knarren weg«. Gleichzeitig keinen der früheren Mitstreiter über die Klinge springen lassen, niemanden verraten; sich also nicht persönliche Vorteile erkaufen, indem man andere verrät, die denselben Weg gegangen sind.

CR: Was jetzt natürlich passiert ist . . .

PS: . . . das war der Grund, weswegen ich mit ihm einen Briefwechsel anfing. Ich wollte diese Haltung der Öffentlichkeit und auch anderen Terroristen bekannt machen, wollte sagen, so geht es vielleicht. Leider hat sich dann später herausgestellt, das Peter-Jürgen Boock nicht mit offenen Karten gespielt hat. In dem Briefwechsel hatte er mir geschrieben: »Ich habe nie einen Menschen getötet und auch niemanden dazu veranlaßt, es zu tun.« Damals habe ich ihm zurückgeschrieben: »Ich habe Dich nie danach gefragt, lieber Peter-Jürgen Boock. Jetzt, da Du das sagst, bleibt mir nichts übrig, als anzunehmen, daß Du die Wahrheit sagst.« In Klammern meinte dieser Satz: Und wenn Du gelogen hast, bist Du ein Schwein! Denn die Lüge bedeutete, das er jemanden, der ihm nicht als Richter oder Staatsanwalt gegenüberstand, sondern als Gesprächspartner und als Freund, in seine Prozeßstrategie einspannte. Denn ich hätte den Briefwechsel auch mit ihm geführt, wenn ich gewußt hätte, daß er ein Mörder ist. Daß er kein Mörder wäre, war für mich nicht die Bedingung des Gesprächs. Aber natürlich ist es eine andere Sache, wenn man es mit einem erklärten Mörder zu tun hat, oder mit einem, der von sich behauptet, daß er fälschlich beschuldigt wird. Und dann stellt sich heraus, daß er gelogen hat. Ich habe das gefürchtet, aber mich selbst gezwungen, ihm zu glauben, sonst hätte ich den Briefwechsel gar nicht weiterführen können. Es war ja nicht nur ein Briefwechsel, sondern eine Freundschaft. Ich bin jahrelang zu ihm hingefahren. Das mache ich übrigens auch heute noch. Ja, irgendwie und halbwegs ist dieser Bruch zwischen uns gekittet.

Zu Paarungen

RW: Bei *Paarungen* merkt man, daß der Roman gewissermaßen aus einer Reihe von Geschichten besteht.

PS: Dieses Reihenprinzip, das Prinzip der Kettengeschichte, habe ich bei E. T. A. Hoffmann ausgeliehen. Bei Hoffmann sind es wirklich autonome Geschichten, die nebeneinanderstehen, untereinander oft überhaupt nicht verbunden. Das ist bei mir nicht so. Das Personal und die Geschichte des Romans sind durch ein gemeinsames Projekt zusammengehalten – eine Wette. Es gibt eine Verkettung von Geschichten, die relativ lose zusammengebunden sind. So ergaben sich für mich akzeptable Teilabschnitte einer langen Strecke, denn ich hatte ja keine Erfahrung mit einem Roman, nur Erfahrung mit Geschichten.

RW: Wie finden Sie die Reaktionen auf den Humor im Roman?

PS: In der *Zeit* hat Iris Radisch behauptet, das Buch habe keinen Funken Humor. In Deutschland scheint es ein ZK zu geben, das darüber bestimmt, wann mit Niveau gelacht werden darf. Denn es steht fest: die Leser haben bei diesem Buch viel gelacht, ganz ohne Lizenz von Iris Radisch. Andere Rezensenten haben übrigens durchaus bemerkt und gelobt, daß eine so ernste Sache wie Trennung hier auf leichtfüßige Weise erzählt wird. Das ist ja – entgegen dem Klischee – gar nicht so neu in Deutschland. Ich gebe zu, daß mir Heinrich Heine oder E. T. A. Hoffmann näher sind als Rilke und George.

CR: Kurt Tucholsky später . . .

PS: Kurt Tucholsky, auch der Poet Bert Brecht. Es gibt tatsächlich eine deutsche Tradition von Ironie, Leichtigkeit, Humor. Es waren vor allem die Juden, die diese Tradition in Gang gehalten haben, die diesen deutschen Tiefsinn immer wieder umgerührt, mit Witz und wunderbaren Gemeinheiten aufgepfeffert haben.

CR: Das ist dann in der Nachkriegsliteratur nahezu verschwunden.

PS: Mit den Juden ist auch diese Tradition fast verschwunden, genauer gesagt, umgebracht worden.

CR: Das Buch ist als eine endgültige Abrechnung mit '68 und mit der sexuellen Revolution der 68er interpretiert worden. Wie stehen Sie dazu?

PS: Ich halte das für ziemlichen Quatsch. Es wäre zu schön, um wahr zu sein, wenn sich die zunehmende Labilität der Ehe-institution auf die verstiegenen Theorien von ein paar 68er-Rebellen zurückführen ließe. Dann wäre das Übel ja sehr leicht zu korri-gieren. Mir scheint aber, daß das Problem vom Facharbeiter hinauf bis ins Haus Windsor empfunden und durchlitten wird. Die Ehe-schwierigkeiten im Haus Windsor sind sicher nicht damit zu er-klären, das man dort zuviel Wilhelm Reich gelesen hat, oder etwa doch?

RW: Jede vierte Ehe in Großbritannien geht inzwischen kaputt . . .

PS: Mein Roman ist ein Versuch, dieses stille, seit 20, 30 Jahren sich aufbauende Erdbeben zu beschreiben, einen Massenvorgang kennt-lich zu machen. Nur weil das alles so ernst ist, ist das Gelächter so bitter nötig.

4

Die Mauern im Kopf –»Es muß einmal . . . ein Ende haben mit dem gekrümmten Gang«

STEPHAN REINHARDT

In einer neulich erschienenen Darstellung der deutschen Nachkriegsliteratur findet sich ein Foto, auf dem zu sehen ist, wie ein junger Mann bei der Verleihung der Berliner Kunstpreise am 18. März 1969 den regierenden Bürgermeister von Berlin, Klaus Schütz, in seiner Rede stört und ihn vom Mikrofon wegdrängt: Peter Schneider.[1] Eine Szene von symbolischer Aussagekraft: Eine neue Generation verweigert das Einverständnis mit der herrschenden Sprachregelung und ihren politischen Sprechern. Bereits im April 1967 während eines sit-ins im Audimax der Freien Universität hatte Peter Schneider in der Rede »Wir haben Fehler gemacht« programmatische Worte für einen neuen Generationenanspruch gefunden: ». . . wir wollen uns jetzt klar ausdrücken. Es geht tatsächlich um die Abschaffung von Ruhe und Ordnung, es geht um undemokratisches Verhalten, es geht darum, endlich nicht mehr sachlich zu sein« (*AN*, 12). Wo die Ordnung ein System schützt, in dem die Menschen in »schlimmen Verhältnissen«[2] leben, ist eine neue Ordnung zu erstreiten, in der mehr Glück möglich sein soll – angesichts dieser so empfundenen Ausgangssituation nicht mehr »sachlich« zu sein, beispielsweise zivilen Ungehorsam zu praktizieren statt repressiver Toleranz, um sich den herrschenden »Verhältnissen« zu widersetzen, schien den Achtundsechzigern das Gebot der Stunde.

Seit Anfang der sechziger Jahre in Berlin Germanistik, Geschichte und Philosophie studierend, begann Peter Schneider ganz »sachlich«: Wie viele Intellektuelle und Gruppe-47-Schriftsteller unterstützte er die Oppositionspartei SPD, in der Hoffnung, sie würde die autoritäre Adenauer-Demokratie endlich ablösen und die Demokratie erneuern. Im Berliner »Wahlkontor« schrieb Schneider 1965 gemeinsam mit Günter Grass, Peter Härtling, Hubert Fichte,

Gudrun Ensslin und Bernward Vesper Reden um und formulierte
Wahlslogans. Die Enttäuschung war groß, als die SPD ein Jahr
später in eine Große Koalition mit der CDU eintrat und sogar die
Verabschiedung der Notstandsgesetze mitbetrieb. In der sich
bildenden »Außerparlamentarischen Opposition« wurde Schneider
in Berlin zu einem der Wortführer des antiautoritären Protestes der
Studenten: Er organisierte die Anti-Springer-Kampagne mit und
stimmte wie Walter Boehlich und Hans Magnus Enzensberger in
den Chor derer ein, für die das Verändern der »schlimmen Verhältnisse«, die schlimmer nicht zu denken waren, den Vorrang vor
allem anderen erhielt. Die Menschen, heißt es in der »Rede an die
deutschen Leser und ihre Schriftsteller«, »gehen aneinander vorbei
und beobachten sich, als wäre jeder der Feind des anderen« (*AN*,
30). Zwar sterben »unsere Arbeiter und Bauern«, lautet der Befund,
nicht an Hunger wie so viele in der Dritten Welt, sie sind noch
schlimmer dran: sie sterben »heimlich an Unterdrückung und
Erniedrigung« (*AN*, 38). Ein Künstler, der seine Phantasie noch
nicht vom »Kapital« hat »zerrütten« lassen, hat folglich »die
Strategie der Befreiung« zu zeigen und für die »Wünsche und Phan-
tasien« »die politische Form« zu suchen – statt den »Kapitalismus«
durch Kunst zu schützen »vor der Rebellion der Wünsche« (*AN*,
38). Unter dem Eindruck des Pariser Mai, der das baldige Bevor-
stehen der Revolution zu verheißen schien, die gesellschaftliche
Besserung der »schlimmen Verhältnisse«, die Einlösung des An-
spruchs auf Glück und Lebenssinn, verstärkte Peter Schneider in
dem *Kursbuch*-Essay »Die Phantasie im Spätkapitalismus und die
Kulturrevolution« noch einmal die Erwartungen: Nicht allein gehe
es nun um »Kulturrevolution«, das heißt um die »Eroberung der
Wirklichkeit durch die Phantasie« (*AP*, 152), sondern um alles:
»Von der Fähigkeit der Studenten, aus ihrer Klasse herauszu-
springen und den Kampf an der Basis zu organisieren, wird es
abhängen, ob die exemplarischen Aktionen in den Klassenkampf
umschlagen« (*AP*, 160).

Als sich bald herausstellte, daß ein Klassenkampf nicht in Sicht
war, korrigierte sich Peter Schneider: Von der Straße führt der Weg
nun in die Wohngemeinschaft, vom Wir zum Ich, von der »politischen Revolte« des Reden- und Flugblätterschreibens zur »literarischen Revolte« (*AP*, 165). »Warst du eigentlich glücklich?« (*L*, 5),
fragt eines Morgens der Student Lenz beim Aufwachen in Peter
Schneiders gleichnamiger Erzählung *Lenz* das Marx-Gesicht auf
dem Plakat seiner Studentenbude – mit dieser Frage (und der

Erzählung *Lenz*) hat Peter Schneider als einer der ersten auf die Desorientierung der Studentenbewegung – ihren Dogmatismus, ihre schematische Begriffssprache – hingewiesen. Im Unterschied zu Büchner, dessen Novelle *Lenz* als Vorlage dient, wird Schneiders Student Lenz nicht wahnsinnig, er leidet vielmehr an der Abstraktheit, der Unsinnlichkeit seines Lebens, an dem theoretischen »Blabla« (*L*, 9) der Freunde, die das (abwesende) revolutionäre Subjekt des Arbeiters idealisieren. Weil Lenz eine politische Idee erst beurteilen kann, wenn er die sie umgebende Wirklichkeit erfahren hat und sich darum die »Welt mit den Sinnen erobern« muß, bricht er aus dem studentischen Milieu theoretischer Selbstbespiegelung aus und läßt sich als Hilfsarbeiter in einer Elektrofirma (wie Schneider selbst 1969 bei Bosch) anstellen. Als indes »die Arbeiter« keineswegs in die gedachte Idealfolie passen, fährt er nach Italien und findet dort in einer norditalienischen Stadt, wonach er gesucht hat: daß Gefühle und Selbsterfahrung keine »bourgeoise Subjektivität« sein müssen, daß zwischen Erkenntnissen und Empfindungen, zwischen Wahrnehmung und Theorie eine Gleichzeitigkeit, ja Übereinstimmung bestehen kann.

Lenz – einer der wenigen literarischen Schlüsseltexte der Studentenbewegung (in 15 Sprachen übersetzt, die deutsche Auflage beträgt 165 000) – ist eine Ermunterung zum Zweifel: nicht nur an den »Verhältnissen«, sondern auch an den eigenen Denkansätzen, und eine Aufforderung, sich alltägliche Bedürfnisse – wie Freundschaft, Körperlichkeit, Solidarität – nicht durch ideologische Vorsätze ausreden zu lassen. Die Warnung vor der Erstarrung des Denkens, das »Menschenrecht auf Irrtum«, auf eigene, neue Erfahrung, werden zu einem tragenden Impuls Peter Schneiders. Das Aufbrechen von Selbstblockade und Selbstzensur, das Entdecken des eigenen Ichumrisses – sie finden bei Peter Schneider ihren Ausdruck auch darin, Widersprüche wahrzunehmen und darzustellen, eingedenk dessen, daß eine zweidimensionale Betrachtungsweise weitaus angemessener ist als eine eindimensionale und daß das Aushalten der nicht *ad hoc* lösbaren Widersprüche und Spannungen der Analyse wirksamere Handlungsimpulse verleiht als dogmatisch geführtes Agieren. Jede Rechthaberei trägt in sich einen autoritären Gestus – sie widerspricht »dem notwendig experimentellen Charakter des politischen Entwurfs« (*DÄ*, 51). Schneider bezieht Literatur und aufklärendes Denken aufeinander als »work in progress«: Es entwickeln sich immer wieder neue Situationen und bilden sich immer wieder neue Erfahrungen, die neue Antworten verlangen.

Mit und seit *Lenz* gibt Peter Schneider der linken »Bewegung« Impulse sowohl durch eingreifende, eingefahrene Gleise stets aufs neue sprengende Essays wie auch als literarischer Chronist aktueller, umstrittener Ereignisse und Vorgänge: 1973 selbst nach dem Ersten Staatsexamen als Referendar wegen angeblich verfassungsfeindlicher Umtriebe vom Berliner Senat abgelehnt, findet er als einziger in . . . *schon bist du ein Verfassungsfeind* (deutsche Auflage: 90 000) eine literarische Form für den Berufsverbotsfall eines Heidelberger Lehrers. »Der Meinung, daß es auch undemokratische Gesetze und Bestimmungen gäbe, bei denen Widerstand, nicht Gehorsam, angebracht sei, kann doch ernsthaft kein Demokrat widersprechen« (*VF*, 30) – diesen Satz eines politisch nicht organisierten Lehrers nimmt die Schulbehörde zum Anlaß, ihn als »Radikalen« aus dem Schuldienst zu entfernen. (Im Briefwechsel mit dem Terroristen Peter-Jürgen Boock versucht er zehn Jahre später eine Brücke zu schlagen zwischen dem Staat und Terrorismus.)[3]

Schneiders Ermunterung zur Souveränität richtet sich auch nach links, etwa als Kritik am feministischen Dogmatismus der zu Beginn der siebziger Jahre die Studentenrevolte fortsetzenden Frauenbewegung (*Die Wette*), und er verteidigt den Einzelnen, der in das Räderwerk der Institutionen und Vorurteile gerät, indem er in dem Filmdrehbuch *Messer im Kopf* schildert, wie ein »Unschuldiger«, der Biochemiker Hoffmann, der von einem Polizisten lebensgefährlich verletzt wurde, fast zerrieben wird von den jeweiligen Interessen: Polizei und Medien machen aus ihm einen Terroristen, für die Linken ist er ein Opfer des Staatsterrors. Mühsam lernt Hoffmann nach dem Kopfschuß (wie Rudi Dutschke) wieder sprechen und ein neues Leben. Auf fruchtbare Weise irritiert Schneider ein ums andere Mal durch ein Denken, das die eigene Wahrnehmung nicht preisgibt, und im Rückblick überrascht, wie sehr dabei der politische Zeitdiagnostiker und Ideenpolitiker im voraus Widersprüche auf den Begriff brachte und in der Formulierung einer aufgeklärten linken Position Recht behielt.

Anfang der achtziger Jahre, als in Polen *Solidarność* das Recht gewerkschaftlicher Selbstorganisation durchzusetzen beginnt, ergeht an die DDR die Aufforderung, Rosa Luxemburgs »Kein Sozialismus ohne Freiheit« endlich in die Tat umzusetzen; an den den Militärputsch von 1980 in Polen als innere Angelegenheit des Landes herunterspielenden SPD-Kanzler Schmidt, an einflußreiche Kommen-

tatoren wie Theo Sommer und Rudolf Augstein richtet Schneider
zugleich die Bitte, nicht die Verletzung des Selbstbestimmungs-
rechtes zu akzeptieren. Wer gegen den Pinochet-Putsch in Chile
protestierte, könne in Sachen Polen nicht schweigen. Wer angesichts
der atomaren Bedrohung das Freiheitsverlangen der Polen über-
gehe, lasse sich auf einen faulen Frieden, einen »Atomfrieden« ein.
Im *Literaturmagazin* stellt Schneider die grundsätzliche Frage:
».. . verliert ein Volk das Recht auf Selbstbestimmung, weil der
Versuch, es einzulösen, ein unerträgliches Risiko darstellt?«[4]

An die Friedensbewegung, die sich in weiten Teilen als »Bewegung zur Vermeidung des Atomkrieges« verstand, ergeht die überraschende, antizyklische Aufforderung, ebenso »eine Bewegung zur
Verhinderung des Atomfriedens« (*DÄ*, 40) zu werden – denn wenn
»›Frieden‹« nur »die Vermeidung einer Katastrophe namens Atom-
krieg« bedeute, was ist er dann noch wert? Schneider bestreitet
nicht, daß »auf dem Feld der Realpolitik« der Satz gilt, »daß es
nichts Wichtigeres gibt als den Frieden« (*DÄ*, 61), Intellektuelle in-
dessen müßten – Schneider argumentiert hier wie Julien Benda in
seinem beeindruckenden Essay »Der Verrat der Intellektuellen«[5] –
»die Aufgabe wahrnehmen, die geschichtliche Wahrheit unab-
hängig von der Frage ihrer politischen Durchsetzbarkeit zu
ermitteln und einzuklagen« (*DÄ*, 61). Früher als andere besteht
Schneider deshalb auch auf der Unteilbarkeit des Selbstbe-
stimmungsrechtes für Osteuropa, und früher als die meisten
entwirft er – 1985 – die Utopie von einem »autonomen Europa, das,
befreit vom Antagonismus der Supermächte, zu einer neuen Einheit
findet« (*DÄ*, 61). Denk- und Warntafeln aufstellend, verteidigt
Schneider den politischen Ansatz der Grünen und der Friedensbewegung und warnt doch zugleich die »ontologische Fraktion«
der Grünen vor der (alten deutschen) philosophischen Glaubens-
haltung, die aus Harmoniebedürfnis die Welt als ein Heiles und
Ganzes denkt und nicht als zutiefst widersprüchlich.[6] Er gibt zu
bedenken, ob das Bild von Manon Maren-Grisebach in ihrer
Philosophie der Grünen, daß der Mensch von Natur aus gut und
Technik das Böse sei, nicht ein Irrtum sein dürfte.[7] Denn das Böse
liegt nicht »außerhalb« des Menschen, sondern gehört zu seinem
»Wesen« anthropologisch hinzu.

Verschwiegenes, Verschwiemeltes, Verschwitztes zur Sprache zu
bringen und Blockdenken aufzubrechen, auf dem Hintergrund dieses dialektischen, antizyklischen Aufklärungs- und Eingreif-Den-
kens ist Peter Schneider einer der wenigen, der sich nicht scheut,

das heiße Eisen der »deutschen Frage« anzufassen. In der DDR
wollte die Bevölkerung die Wiedervereinigung, aber durfte nicht
darüber sprechen; in der Bundesrepublik wollte man sie nicht
mehr, sprach aber an Festtagen so darüber, als ob man sie wollte.
Zwar war in die Verfassung der BRD das »Wiedervereinigungs-
gebot« eingeschrieben, die Feierreden aber glichen der »1001.
Aufführung eines Repertoire-Theaters«, an der niemand mehr
Anteil nahm. Die Geschichte dieser fortschreitenden Trennung
führte mit der Zeit zu zwei »Lebenskulturen« und Staaten; wer also
die Vereinigung wirklich wollte, dem, so Schneider, war ein »von
der Mauer befreiter Staaten-Bund ›BDDR‹« vorzuschlagen, ein
Staaten-Bund, der in einem friedlichen Systemwettbewerb den
Besseren ermittelt (*DÄ*, 28). Nur ein dritter Weg, ein »Misch-
system«, in dem Freiheit und soziale Gerechtigkeit miteinander
verbunden würden, vermag, betont Schneider, der »Utopie von
einer menschengerechten Gesellschaft« nahezukommen (*DÄ*, 29).

Zu einem Zeitpunkt, als so gut wie keiner an ein baldiges Ende
der Mauer dachte, sammelte Peter Schneider, der sich ebenso mit
der Teilung abgefunden hatte wie die allermeisten, Geschichten
und Anekdoten, in denen sie überwunden wurde: durch »Mauerspringer«. Phantasie – die ins Blaue hinein eine Möglichkeit beschreibt – bricht auf, was für immer festbetoniert scheint. Auf seiner Reporterreise *Der Mauerspringer* (deutsche Auflage ca. 50 000;
in 17 Sprachen übersetzt) durch deutsch-deutsches Bewußtsein und
Befinden in den getrennten Stadthälften Berlins trifft Schneider immer wieder auf die Mauer in den Köpfen, auf Verhaltensweisen,
Denk- und Gefühlsprägungen, die der jeweilige Staat zementiert
hat: Staat und Einzelner, Kollektiv und Individuum, Über-Ich und
Ich – ihr Verhältnis hat eine je nach Stadtteil jeweils eigene Fär-
bung. Schneider findet dafür den – voraussehenden, nach der Vereinigung bestätigten – Satz: »Die Mauer im Kopf einzureißen wird
länger dauern, als irgendein Abrißunternehmen für die sichtbare
Mauer braucht« (*DMS*, 102).

Noch bevor die Mauer sich dann am 9. November 1989 tatsächlich öffnete, hatte Peter Schneider bereits im März/April desselben
Jahres in einem Aufsatz für die *New York Times* auf die Frage geant-
wortet »Was wäre, wenn die Mauer fällt« und vorausgesagt:
». . . die Mauer bröselt schon . . . die Mauer wird dieses Jahr-
tausend, vielleicht sogar die Wochen, die zwischen der Ver-
fertigung und Veröffentlichung dieses Artikels vergehen, nicht
überleben«.[8] Schneiders erstaunliche Voraussage der Maueröffnung

vom Frühjahr 1989 zielt nicht auf »Wiedervereinigung«, sondern –
wie 1982 in der *Frankfurter Rundschau* vorgeschlagen – auf eine
»schrittweise Konföderation« (*EM*, 175) zwischen den beiden
deutschen Staaten, deren Bewohner in vierzig Jahren Trennung
ebenso viele Unterschiede wie Gemeinsamkeiten ausgebildet haben:
Auf diesem dritten Weg könne endlich jeder der beiden Staaten im
freien Wettbewerb zeigen, »wer was besser kann«, vorausgesetzt,
beide geben die »These von der grundsätzlichen Überlegenheit des
einen Lebensmodells über das andere« auf (*EM*, 175). Nur so, hebt
Schneider hervor, könne es zu einem »freien Wettbewerb zwischen
zwei Lebensweisen unter einigermaßen vergleichbaren Bedingungen« kommen (*EM*, 175).

Während Helmut Schmidt am 22. September 1989 in der *Zeit*
feststellt, daß eine »Eruption in der DDR« den Reformprozeß im
Ostblock gefährden und daß die deutsche Frage »erst im nächsten
Jahrhundert gelöst werden« wird,[9] befindet sich Peter Schneider auf
einer Amerikareise, in Hanover, New Hampshire, und erfährt dort
am 9. November 15 Uhr Ortszeit, daß die Mauer geöffnet worden
ist. Das Mauerspringen wurde für ein paar Tage zum fröhlichen
Massensport. Im Unterschied zu vielen, den meisten Linken und Li-
beralen von den Grünen bis zur SPD, reagierte Schneider spontan
zustimmend zu dem »politischen Wunder« der Maueröffnung:
»Was, wenn nicht Freude sollen die Deutschen empfinden, wenn
diese Mauer, von Anfang an eine Notmaßnahme und Mißgeburt,
auf friedliche Weise fällt? Was immer die nun offene Tür an alten
und neuen Konflikten sichtbar machen wird, der neue Zustand ist
unendlich besser als der alte« (*EM*, 10).

Die Zustimmung verstellt Schneider indes nicht den Blick für die
neuen Probleme. Weitsichtig diagnostiziert er angesichts der neuen
Güterverteilung den bald beispiellos ausbrechenden Fremdenhaß
und Rassismus: »Es wird die nächste und wichtigste Aufgabe sein,
die Rechte dieser Ausländer zu verteidigen und zu erweitern« (*EM*,
11). Was wird werden aus dem vereinten Deutschland, dem nun
bevölkerungsreichsten Land Europas in der Mitte des Kontinents
und der drittgrößten Industrienation? Schneider stellt in dem Essay
»Gibt es zwei deutsche Kulturen?« (geschrieben im Mai 1990; siehe
EM, 120–56) ein Gedankenspiel an: Wird die Vereinigung ein
Schnitt sein, anläßlich dessen 1990 wieder angeknüpft wird –
»Kühlschranktheorie« von ihm genannt – an die nach 1945 in der
DDR vereisten alten deutschen Eigenschaften und Eigenarten? Oder
hat – eine »Feldtheorie« – das jeweilige kulturelle Milieu die

Menschen verändert? In der Sprache der Zwillingsforschung: Bedeutet die Prägungskraft der Gene, daß nach dem Auftauen des Eisschranks wieder angeknüpft wird an den »Nationalcharakter« und alte »Traditionen«? Der Ausbruch der »nationalen Passionen und Marotten«, der Bürgerkriege und Massaker im Namen »nationalistischer und rassistischer Ressentiments« in Ost- und Mitteleuropa scheint, stellt Schneider fest, die »Kühlschranktheorie« zu bestätigen. Das »nationale Selbstgefühl« wird allenthalben gehegt und gepflegt. Schneider besteht den unglaublichen Wettlauf mit der Zeit, indem er die Entwicklung richtig voraussagt: eine hohe Arbeitslosigkeit, die sozialen Sprengstoff in sich birgt, der sich »als Potential für rechtsextreme Populisten erweisen« wird. Wird Rückkehr zur Normalität im Sinne einer Kühlschranktheorie auch bedeuten, daß die vereinten Deutschen wieder einen ökonomischen Größenwahn entwickeln werden, der gewaltsame Eroberungen gar nicht mehr nötig hat, weil er sich wirtschaftlich selbst alles zu Füßen legt – wird das nicht die Ängste der Nachbarn nähren? Schneider gibt der optimistischeren Version der Feldtheorie den Vorzug, nämlich daß Normalisierung bedeuten sollte, daß die Deutschen normaler werden, das heißt: »selbstbewußter im großzügigen Sinn des Wortes, toleranter, fremdenfreundlicher, lustiger, kurz . . . glücklicher« (*EM*, 156).

Peter Schneider macht sich in den Wochen und Monaten nach der Wende zu einem Sprachrohr des »Umdenkens«. Der Zusammenbruch des realen Sozialismus bedeutet für ihn die »größte Herausforderung an das linke Denken«. In einer Rede bei einem »Kulturtreff« (im Januar 1990) in der Ostberliner Akademie der Künste (und in einem gleichzeitigen Interview für *L'Unità*, das die *taz* wenige Tage später nachdruckt) stellt er die Frage: »Was heißt jetzt noch Sozialismus?«, und drängt auf Begriffsklärung und Überprüfung des Sozialismus-Modells. Soll, fragt er, der zu dieser Zeit ins Gespräch gekommene Begriff der »sozialistischen Marktwirtschaft« (oder der ältere Begriff »demokratischer Sozialismus«) noch »Vergesellschaftung von Produktionsmitteln« bedeuten, was nach der Ostblock-Erfahrung ausscheide, oder »gesellschaftliche Kontrolle über die Produktion«? Dann aber wäre es redlicher, stellt er fest, von »sozial gezähmtem Kapitalismus« zu reden.[10]

Während er im *taz*-Interview[11] noch einmal betont, das Marx' Kritik am Kapitalismus »nichts an Gültigkeit verloren« habe, weil eine Alternative zum »kapitalistischen System« zu »wollen« sei, gibt er diese Sprache wenig später auf. Obwohl er *L'Unitá* und *taz* noch zu Protokoll gibt, daß das »Scheitern des realen Sozialismus« nicht berechtigt, »den endgültigen Sieg des Kapitalismus zu erklären«, gibt er wenige Monate später in der *Zeit* dagegen jenen Recht, die den Sozialismus schon immer »für einen Irrweg der menschlichen Zivilisation« gehalten haben.[12] »Kann einem in diesen Tagen nicht der Verdacht kommen, die Geschichte höchstselbst habe im Zweikampf zwischen Sozialismus und Kapitalismus entschieden und den letzteren zum Sieger erkoren? Und dieser Sieger spricht nun vom Berg Sinai zu uns herab: Du sollst kein anderes Wirtschaftssystem haben neben mir!? Ich gratuliere allen, die derartige Anfechtungen nicht kennen«.[13]

In einer »Überprüfung eines Szenarios« überschriebenen Nachbetrachtung vom Sommer 1990 zu den deutschlandpolitischen Essays *Extreme Mittellage* (mit der für einen Essayband in der Erstausgabe hohen Auflage von 13 000 Exemplaren) erteilt Schneider dem dritten Weg eine endgültige Absage: »Auch wenn man die Hand noch solange gegen das erst von Osten und dann von Westen einfallende Licht an die Stirn hält, im Schnittpunkt der Lichtstrahlen wird sich ein neuer Weg nicht zeigen« (*EM*, 182). Mit Recht, scheint mir, verteidigt der gelernte Mehrschritt- und Vorausdenker Peter Schneider in einem »Plädoyer für eine Vergangenheitsbewältigung der Linken« ausdrücklich das von ihm selbst in Anspruch genommene »Recht zum Umdenken und . . . auf Irrtum und Widerruf« als »eines der vornehmsten Menschenrechte«.[14] Gedanken sind frei, und Zeiten ändern sich und verlangen neue Fragen und Antworten.

Ist aber, sei gefragt, mit dem Sieg des Kapitalismus über den real existierenden Sozialismus die soziale (sozialistische?) Idee, der Streit darüber, was soziale Gerechtigkeit bedeutet, tatsächlich aus der Welt geschafft? Ist der derzeitige Privatisierungsfundamentalismus in jedem Falle und für alle Zeit der Weisheit letzter Schluß? Ist eine gerechtere Verteilung erwirtschafteter Güter zwischen reichen Industrieländern und armen Drittweltländern schon aus Gründen gemeinsamer ökologischer Zwangshaftung nicht ein Gebot der Vernunft? Wie es Peter Schneider selbst noch 1980 in seinem eindrucksvollen Südamerika-Bericht »Die Botschaft des Pferdekopfs« in dem Satz zusammengefaßt hat: »Der Umschlag von der Beherrschung der Natur in ihre Zerstörung kann nur von den Ländern aufgehalten werden, die diesen Prozeß in Gang gesetzt haben« (*BP*, 53). Erfordert das ökologische Überlebensinteresse auf Dauer nicht eine (weltweit) gemeinwohlorientierte Zähmung aggressiver Kapitalentfaltung, also Sozialismus im Kapitalismus, das heißt ständiges

Nachdenken über einen dritten Weg? Weil über dergleichen nicht mehr nachgedacht wird in dem Essayband *Extreme Mittellage*, erkennt Stefan Berkholz in seiner *Zeit*-Rezension in der »beinahe vollständigen Anerkennung des florierenden Kapitalismus« einen »Offenbarungseid für die kritische Intelligenz«.[15]

Wenn Klaus Hartung (in seinem Essay »Neunzehnhundertneunundachtzig«, 1990) davon gesprochen hat, daß die »größte Chance für sozialistisches Denken heute« in dem Versuch liege, »sich zum bewußten Teil des radikalen Scheiterns zu machen«, dann bleibt die Frage offen und zu beantworten: ob »sozialistisches Denken heute« auf soziale und ökologische Modelle verzichten kann?[16] Hat es, sei weiter gefragt, mit Vergangenheitsbewältigung zu tun, wenn Schneider schreibt, »die Linke« habe »niemals gründlich« »die lang geübte Schonhaltung, die Stalins Lager als einen ›Fehler‹ qualifizierte«, »revidiert« (*EM*, 60)? Und war es so, wie Schneider in dem Essay »Überprüfung eines Szenarios« behauptet, daß ein Konsens der westdeutschen Linken gegenüber der DDR in der Meinung bestanden habe: »Der reale Sozialismus in der DDR, auch wenn er noch so kritikwürdig ist, stellt eine historische Chance für die Deutschen dar, die einzig konsequente Antwort auf den Nazifaschismus« (*EM*, 178)? Und daß darum die Linke den »antiautoritären Impetus und die Forderung nach direkter Demokratie« hinsichtlich der DDR zur Gänze der Rechten überlassen habe (*EM*, 181)? Ist die behauptete Identifizierung der »Linken« mit dem »Osten« nicht ein neuer Irrtum? War es nicht vielmehr so, daß – von DKP und SEW-West und ein paar dogmatischen Splittergrüppchen abgesehen – die »Linke« den Stalinismus und Sowjetmarxismus strikt abgelehnt hat: von Marcuse, Adorno und Habermas bis zu Dutschke, von Böll bis Grass? Immer wieder hat »die Linke« darauf hingewiesen – 1956, 1968, 1970 und 1980 – daß der unfreie DDR-Sozialismus doch gerade den antiautoritären, direkten demokratischen »Impetus« verweigert?

Schneider läßt zu Recht – sich Poppers Gedanken zu eigen machend, daß das Vertuschen von Irrtümern »die größte intellektuelle Sünde« (*EM*, 57) sei – der in der Regel zur Arroganz neigenden Intellektuellenzunft nichts durchgehen, andererseits greift er ins Füllhorn des Populismus, wenn er die Intellektuellen zu den »gefährlichsten« »Arten« (*EM*, 74) zählt: Was sie sich in ihrer Realitätsblindheit an Utopien ausdächten, sei das Geschäft des Verführers, der die anderen die Zeche zahlen lasse; im Namen ihrer Ideen würden gesellschaftliche Verbrechen begangen. Gewiß gibt es so etwas wie einen idealistischen Affekt, der »Opium für Intellektuelle« (Raymond Aron, 1955)[17] ist, was wäre andererseits die Welt aber ohne Ideen und Ideale – wie zum Beispiel denen von einer sozialen Gerechtigkeit oder ökologischen Verträglichkeit? Die Tatsache, daß es perniziöse Ideen – Rassismus, Nationalismus – gibt, befreit keinen Intellektuellen von der Pflicht, bessere zu denken: Toleranz zum Beispiel.

Reißt der politische Publizist Peter Schneider, sei weiter gefragt, Mauern im Kopf ein, wenn er in seinem Golfkriegsartikel von einem »Desaster« anläßlich des »ersten außenpolitischen Testes der neuen Bundesrepublik« spricht und dies unter anderem mit dem Satz begründet: »Festzuhalten bleibt dies: die Bedrohung Israels wird vom Bewußtsein und Unterbewußtsein der deutschen Friedensbewegung ausgeblendet«?[18] War es so? War nicht vielmehr Opfer gleich Opfer? Und darum der Wunsch vorherrschend, die Kriegsschwelle zu erhöhen durch humanere politische Mittel als einen Krieg?

Folgt der politische Essayist Peter Schneider auch dem populistischen Argument, daß die linke, liberale Pädagogik an den Mordbrennereien von Mölln vor allem mitschuldig sei, weil sie, wie er in seiner *Kursbuch*-Betrachtung »Erziehung nach Mölln« schreibt,[19] von der These, daß der Mensch gut sei, ausgehe, statt das in jedem Menschen vorhandene Gewalt- und Aggressionspotential anzuerkennen und entsprechend zu reagieren? Sagen nicht auch »linke« Pädagogen, daß der Mensch anthropologisch ebenso gut wie schlecht ist und daß Pädagogik gerade auch das Aggressionspotential zu zivilisieren hat? Hat das Fernsehen durch seine Bilder von den brennenden Häusern in Rostock-Lichtenhagen und Mölln der Gewaltwelle wirklich Auftrieb gegeben, wie Schneider meint,[20] oder war und ist dafür mitverantwortlich nicht eher eine andere Ereigniskette: die Relativierung der deutschen Verbrechen im Dritten Reich durch den Historikerstreit; das Ausbleiben einer Verfassungsdiskussion, in der der zur Bundesrepublik beitretenden DDR-Bevölkerung, zumal den Jugendlichen und Arbeitslosen, die freiheitlichen, westlichen Grundgedanken der Verfassung schmackhaft gemacht worden wären; ferner ein Rassisten ermunternder Umgang mit dem Asylgesetz; die deutschnationale Variante der Wir-sind-wieder-Wer-Stimmung, eine spürbare Bewegung nach rechts mit der Rehabilitierung angeblich ganz unschuldiger Begriffe wie Nation und Volk.

Eduard Hoffmann, die Hauptfigur in Peter Schneiders erstem, zum Teil kurzweilig und witzig erzähltem Roman *Paarungen* (deutsche Auflage: 46 000; bereits in sieben Sprachen übersetzt), ist ein Intellektueller, der als Naturwissenschaftler Karriere macht und seine alten Auffassungen revidiert hat. Einst ein Achtundsechziger, bevorzugt Eduard nun in dem alten Dauerstreit, ob für das menschliche Verhalten vor allem Erbfaktoren oder das Milieu verantwortlich zu machen seien, das biologische Erklärungsmodell – was ihm sein Bruder Lothar zum Vorwurf macht. Mit ihm, noch immer ein Achtundsechziger, liegt er im »Urstreit« – ein Streit über die jeweiligen Ergebnisse der Zwillingsforschung, der sich auf witzige, unterhaltende Weise durch den Roman zieht.

Eine Ideen- und Bewußtseins-Bilanz ziehend, zeichnet Peter Schneider in *Paarungen* das Porträt der »Söhne und Töchter der Nazigeneration«, die »unter einem Unschuldskomplex« leiden: »Nie zuvor war eine Generation durch die Geschichte derart verführt wie die unsere, die eigenen Eltern total schuldig und sich selbst total unschuldig zu sprechen. Was haben wir davon außer ewiger Unmündigkeit? Noch als längst Erwachsene schleifen wir unsere Eltern an den Haaren hinter uns her und geben ihnen die Schuld dafür, daß wir nicht so geworden sind, wie wir werden wollten« (*P*, 120). Auf diesen Generationenbefund negativer Fixierung folgt wie in Hanns-Josef Ortheils thematisch verwandtem Roman *Abschied von den Kriegsteilnehmern* die Aufforderung zum Erwachsenwerden: »Selbst wenn sich alle unsere Schwächen als . . . Spätfolgen einer unbewältigten Vergangenheit ausweisen ließen, einmal, irgendwann in unserem Leben müssen wir sie annehmen und behaupten, daß es unsere sind« (*P*, 120).

Die eigenen Schwächen zu akzeptieren, indem man mit ihnen umgehen lernt, gehört zum Erwachsenwerden von Individuen, Gruppen und Staaten hinzu. Kann diese Rückkehr des Achtundsechzigers Peter Schneiders zur »Normalität«, sein langer Marsch von Marx zu Popper, bedeuten, daß im Sinne seiner Kühlschranktheorie an die alten deutschen Traditionen wieder angeknüpft wird: an Volk, Nation und angeblichen Nationalcharakter? Das wäre wieder der Irrweg des deutschen Sonderwegs. Ist nicht vielmehr allen geholfen, wenn wir mit Peter Schneider seiner Feldtheorie folgen, derzufolge wir uns alle »selbstbewußter« wünschen, das heißt »toleranter, fremdenfreundlicher, lustiger« (*EM*, 156). Dabei die freiheitlichen, republikanischen Verfassungswerte der Demokratie als Verfassungspatrioten auf dem intellektuellen Meinungsmarkt auszurufen, bekommt allen besser als das dumpfe: »Ich bin stolz, ein Deutscher zu sein«. Dergleichen »Identität« krümmt den Gang wieder und errichtet nur wieder Mauern und Stacheldrahtzäune in den Köpfen.[21]

Anmerkungen

[1] Volker Bohn (Hg.), *Deutsche Literatur seit 1945* (Frankfurt am Main, Suhrkamp, 1993).

[2] Peter Schneider, »Rede an die deutschen Leser und ihre Schriftsteller«, *AN*, 29–38, hier: S. 31.

[3] Siehe Peter Schneider und Peter-Jürgen Boock, *Ratte – tot. Ein Briefwechsel* (Darmstadt und Neuwied, Luchterhand, 1985).

[4] Peter Schneider, »Über das allmähliche Verschwinden einer Himmelsrichtung. Variationen über das Thema ›Der Intellektuelle und die Macht‹«, *Literaturmagazin*, 16 (1985), 48–59, nachgedruckt in *DÄ*, 54–64; hier: 59.

[5] Vgl. Julien Benda, *La Trahison des Clercs* (Paris, Bernard Grasset, 1927).

[6] Siehe »Keine Lust aufs grüne Paradies«, *DÄ*, 41–53, hier: S. 44. Ursprünglich veröffentlicht im *Kursbuch*, 74 (1983), 180–88.

[7] Manon Maren-Grisebach, *Philosophie der Grünen* (München, Olzog Verlag, 1982).

[8] Dieser Artikel erschien zuerst im *New York Times Magazine*, 25. Juni 1989, dann in der *taz*, 14. November 1989, schließlich 1990 in *EM*, 157–76.

[9] Zitiert nach: Peter Schneider, »Was wäre, wenn die Mauer fällt«, *taz*, 14. November 1989, S. 11–12.

[10] »Was heißt jetzt noch Sozialismus? Rede beim Kulturtreff in der Ostberliner Akademie der Künste«, *Süddeutsche Zeitung*, 13./14. Januar 1990, 190.

[11] »›Es riecht nach östlichem Elend‹. Der Westberliner Schriftsteller Peter Schneider hält die deutsche Vereinigung für unvermeidbar und Marx' Kritik am Kapitalismus für wichtiger denn je«, *taz*, 22. Januar 1990, 10. Das Interview war am 19. Januar in *L'Unità* erschienen.

[12] Peter Schneider, »Man kann sogar ein Erdbeben verpassen. Plädoyer für eine Vergangenheitsbewältigung der Linken«, *Die Zeit*, 27. April 1990, 57, nachgedruckt in ungekürzter Form in *EM*, 54–78.

[13] Ebd.

[14] Ebd.

[15] Stefan Berkholz, »Ratlos wie die meisten. Peter Schneiders Plädoyer für eine Kultur des Zweifels«, *Die Zeit*, 5. Oktober 1990, 35–36.

[16] Klaus Hartung, *Neunzehnhundertneunundachtzig*, hrsg. von Freimut Duwe (Darmstadt, Luchterhand Literaturverlag, 1990).

[17] Vgl. Raymond Aron, *L'Opium des Intellectuels* (Paris, Calmann-Lévy, 1955).

[18] Peter Schneider, »Das falsche gute Gewissen der Friedensbewegung«, *Frankfurter Allgemeine Zeitung*, 19. April 1991, 36.

¹⁹ Peter Schneider, »Erziehung nach Mölln«, *Kursbuch*, 113 (1993), 131–41. Dieser Essay erschien in kürzerer und anderer Fassung in der *Frankfurter Allgemeinen Zeitung*, 7. September 1993 unter dem Titel »›Es will dich hier niemand ausgrenzen, Arno!‹«, und in *VEG*, 33–56, unter dem Titel »Vom dünnen Firnis der Zivilisation«.
²⁰ Ebd., 113, 138.
²¹ Vgl. hierzu »Das Ende der Befangenheit?«, *DÄ*, 65–81. Das im Titel meines Aufsatzes angeführte Zitat entstammt *DÄ*, 81.

5

'Ein gewisses Maß subjektiver Verzweiflung . . .': Peter Schneider's *Lenz*

RHYS W. WILLIAMS

In 'Die Beseitigung der ersten Klarheit', which forms a particularly revealing autobiographical 'Nachwort' to Peter Schneider's *Atempause. Versuch, meine Gedanken über Literatur und Kunst zu ordnen* (1977), the author recalls the stay in Italy which formed at least part of the inspiration for the Italian episode in *Lenz*. It was a stay which saw the completion of the political essay 'Die Phantasie im Spätkapitalismus und die Kulturrevolution', the most theoretical of Schneider's essays on politics. Yet his sojourn in the Albani hills was also marked by personal emotion: 'Gleichzeitig hatte ich eine Trennung hinter mir, mit der ich nicht fertig wurde' (*AP*, 230). Looking back on that period, Schneider is struck precisely by that intermingling of the personal and the public, the emotional and the intellectual, which characterizes his evocation of the period in *Lenz*. 'Es kann sein', he reflects, 'daß ein gewisses Maß subjektiver Verzweiflung notwendig ist, um für die Verzweiflung anderer gesellschaftlicher Gruppen empfindlich zu werden' (*AP*, 230). For Schneider (and, as I shall argue, for Lenz) it is the personal crisis which triggers the political dilemma, and it is as much to resolve intensely private questions that the political analysis is undertaken. Indeed, the more intense the suffering, the more strenuous and abstract are the intellectual efforts required to dissect and fix the emotional impulses. The interrelationship of the psychological and the social does not merely constitute an essential thematic strand of the text, as has frequently been noted;[1] it also informs the very structure of the story, conditions the use of motifs and accounts for the presence of apparently trivial incidents.

In the opening section of *Lenz*, the first of forty-three such sections, Schneider presents a dream sequence which signals to the reader the intertwining of the political and the private. Lenz wakes after what is described as one of his 'habitual' dreams: he and L. (the girlfriend whose departure has prompted his emotional crisis) are borne along inside a dark tunnel; Lenz then falls hundreds of feet and is taken up on a conveyor belt to be received by a waiting group: 'Frauen mit riesigen Brüsten, Zauberer, Clowns, salto-schlagende Kinder, die ganze kaputte Fellinitruppe' (L, 5). A man kisses him on the mouth; enraged, Lenz wakes, only to confront the picture of Marx hanging above his bed with the question: 'Was waren deine Träume, alter Besserwisser, nachts meine ich? Warst du eigentlich glücklich?' (L, 5). The dream of falling, which betokens anxiety, the unexplained disappearance of L. from the dream, the echo of Fellini, in which the experiences of childhood return to confront the adult, all these point to Lenz's emotional crisis. But elements of the dream also have a structural significance: the industrial setting points forward to Lenz's encounter with the world of work, the male kiss prefigures an incident with B. in Italy, while the Fellini reference points up the significance of the cinema as a frame of reference for incidents in the story and adumbrates the Italian journey which Lenz will undertake. Moreover, the juxtaposition of the dream and the question addressed to Marx raises the central question of the relationship between political analysis and emotional fulfilment, between politics and psychology, a question which places Schneider's work firmly in the context of the student movement of the early 1970s.

The first twenty-five sections of the text present Lenz's attempts in Berlin to overcome the dissociation of sensibility from which he suffers. We glimpse Lenz in a variety of encounters: with Dieter, a fellow member of the political workshop (Section 5), with Marina (Sections 6, 12, 14 and 22), who offers temporary sexual gratification, with Walter, an old schoolfriend and social misfit (Section 10), with a famous writer who bears an uncanny similarity to Günter Grass (Section 16), with Wolfgang, a genuinely working-class member of the workshop (Section 19), with his former girl-friend L. (Section 21), a meeting which finally seals the end of the relationship, and with B. (Section 23), a father-figure who is to reappear in an Italian episode. In addition, some sections present Lenz in isolation (sections 1–4, 8, 11, 13, 18), in the world of work (Sections 7, 9, 13), at demonstrations (Section 15), at political meetings (Section 17), and at a party (Section 20). The crisis is presented on the one hand as being a psychological, or even an epistemological one, on the other as an expression of a specifically

socio-political dilemma. Schneider's strenuous efforts to fuse these
perspectives are not always successful.

Lenz's crisis, while it is prompted by the break-up of his
relationship with L., swiftly assumes the quality of a wider
existential one, reminiscent of Handke's *Die Angst des Tormanns
beim Elfmeter*, and via Handke, of Sartre's *La Nausée* and a tradition
of German literature stretching back to Hofmannsthal's so-called
Chandos-Brief. The crisis is variously presented as a dissociation of
sensibility, as a linguistic disjunction, a disruption of the relationship between signified and signifier. Observing the rush-hour
bustle, Lenz perceives his social isolation in epistemological terms:
'Sie gehen zur Arbeit, dachte Lenz. Er verband mit dem Satz keine
Vorstellung' (*L*, 6). This dilemma is easily resolved, of course; all
Lenz would need to do would be to find employment, and this is
precisely what he does. Yet the dissociation of sensibility refuses to
be confined to a minor matter of employment. His inability to
respond conventionally to stimuli is presented as a wider
epistemological problem:

> Nach ein paar Stationen stieg Lenz um. Der Bahnhof war alt, fast eine
> Ruine. Zwischen Gleisen, die nicht mehr befahren wurden, wucherte
> Gras. Büsche wuchsen an abgestellten Waggons hoch, das Laub hing
> über Dächer und Fenster, in der Luft ein schwerer Geruch. Wie von
> Kastanienbäumen im Frühling, dachte Lenz, sah dann, daß da
> tatsächlich Kastanienbäume waren. (*L*, 7)

The echoes of Handke (and of Sartre's *La Nausée* with its chestnut
tree in the public park) are unmistakable. Yet Schneider's scene has
two further ingredients. The landscape itself is neither irrelevant
nor arbitrary; it is also a political landscape, the cityscape of a
divided Berlin, in which the overgrown state of the railway track
in West Berlin signals the disputed jurisdiction over the GDR-
owned S-Bahn. The scene has a further function in that it triggers
for Lenz a childhood memory, for the above quotation continues:

> Er sah eine abschüssige Straße vor sich, es war die Stadt, in der er
> aufgewachsen war. Mit dem Rad fuhr er unter den Kastanienbäumen
> hindurch. Die Äste bildeten ein Dach über die Straße, und der verbotene
> Samengeruch, den er sich morgens nach dem Aufstehen von den
> Händen wusch, strömte von den Blättern herab und verfolgte ihn bis
> vor das Schultor. (*L*, 7)

The scene acquires thus a multiple meaning. It is employed to signal a heightened state of awareness, a distortion of normal perception. Yet it also operates in a traditional symbolic manner, evoking through its smell the guilt of childhood sexuality. The chestnut trees are both arbitrary, mere signs to which Lenz struggles to attribute meaning, and profoundly significant, the instrument by which childhood memories are evoked by a kind of Proustian 'mémoire involontaire'.

Examples of disturbed perceptions abound, particularly in the early sections of the text, and were no doubt responsible for the tendency of critics to ascribe *Lenz* to the 'Neue Subjektivität' of the 1970s. On his journey into the city in the third section, Lenz 'stellte sich vor, daß die Häuser und Straßen auf Schienen an ihm vorüber rollten' (*L*, 6). This perhaps not uncommon experience is followed by a sudden phenomenological insight into the essence of objects: 'Er wunderte sich über die Helligkeit, die jeden Gegenstand besonders hervorhob. Die Fenster der oberen Stockwerke, die Baumkronen, die von hier oben wie Büsche aussahen, die Autobahnen unter dem Zug, alles, als sähe er es zum ersten Mal' (*L*, 6). The disturbance in his normal perception of things is reflected in the sudden changes of scale: 'Als er die Zeitung aufschlug, sah er die Zähne des Reißverschlusses an seinem Mantel. Sie kamen ihm zu groß vor' (*L*, 6); later, during his meeting with B., Lenz admits that he is incapable of political action because of his inability to form a coherent picture of the world; his world has fragmented into a series of unconnected and disturbing perceptions: 'Ich habe den bösen Blick, ich sehe schon alles wie durch ein Vergrößerungsglas, das mir nur noch Widerwärtigkeiten zeigt' (*L*, 49). Significantly, this sense of heightened perception is presented as an inhibiting factor to political involvement. Far from offering aesthetic or epistemological compensations, Lenz's states of heightened awareness are presented as isolating him from his social milieu, as threatening his relationships and undermining his political resolve.

It is hardly surprising that three sections which depict Lenz alone in Berlin should not only best illustrate his heightened awareness, but contain the most specific references to Büchner's *Lenz*. Büchner's text is employed almost exclusively to reinforce Lenz's disturbed mental state and direct allusions are not found later than the twenty-eighth of the forty-three sections. Once Lenz begins to encounter Roman society, even before his move to Trento,

depictions of extreme mental states are less in evidence. In the
eighth section, Lenz wakes in the night and, obsessed by images of
L., wanders around the city: 'Dann fing er an zu rennen . . . Als
Lenz zurückging, war die Angst weg, er fühlte sich leicht' (*L*, 12),
lines which supply an obvious echo of Büchner's lines: 'Es faßte ihn
eine namenlose Angst . . . Er riß sich auf und flog den Abhang
hinunter . . . Er sah Lichter, es wurde ihm leichter.'[2] The twelfth
section depicts an incident in which Lenz wanders alone along a
Berlin canal in the twilight: 'Einmal sah er das Gesicht eines
Vorübergehenden mit so großer Deutlichkeit, daß es ihm die
Tränen in die Augen trieb' (*L*, 17). The gradual loss of contours, the
disappearance at dusk of the 'Grenze zwischen Dächern und
Himmel' (*L*, 18), prompt in him first an attempt to control his
sense-impressions by throwing stones into the canal so as to shatter
the reflections of the houses in the water, and then a feeling of utter
desolation: '. . . und alles so kalt, so steinern. Es wurde ihm
entsetzlich einsam, er war allein, er wollte mit sich sprechen, er
konnte nicht, er wagte kaum zu atmen' (*L*, 18). The quotation from
Büchner's *Lenz* here is verbatim.[3] Apart from two brief quotations:
'er hatte sich ganz vergessen' (*L*, 22), when Lenz is drawn into a
political debate in the factory, and 'er wurde ruhig' (*L*, 23) after
Marina offers him sexual gratification, the direct Büchner allusions
are confined to a section in which Lenz observes a group of
window-shoppers eagerly examining the latest Volkswagen models.
Again it is his sense of social isolation which is stressed:

> Er ging weiter, es wurde ihm unbehaglich, er fühlte sich ausge-
> schlossen . . . Eine sonderbare Angst befiel ihn, er hätte der Sonne
> nachlaufen mögen . . . Er klammerte sich an alle Gegenstände, Gestalten
> zogen rasch vorbei, er drängte sich an sie . . . er schrie, er sang, er
> wollte sich kleiner machen. (*L*, 32–3)

The last three sentences of this passage are direct quotations.[4] Only
once in the Italian sections of the story is the Büchner model
referred to, a reference which characteristically occurs right at the
beginning of the Italian journey. In the Albani hills, Lenz experiences a sudden sense of alienation and loneliness:

> Er stellte sich vor, daß er morgen allein aufwachen würde. Er rannte
> hinaus in den Wind, die Wolken flogen dunkel und rasend wie die
> Gespenster in seinem Innern, er lief den Hang hinunter, es war ihm als
> ob die Hügel sich hoben und senkten . . . (*L*, 56)

There is a faint echo here of Büchner's lines: 'es verschmolz ihm alles in eine Linie, wie eine steigende und sinkende Welle, zwischen Himmel und Erde, es war ihm als läge er an einem unendlichen Meer, das leise auf- und abwogte'.[5] While mountainous scenery triggers heightened states of awareness for Büchner's Lenz (a situation which is echoed in Schneider's text in the above example) it ceases to provoke crises for Schneider's central character, even though mountains form the backcloth for the whole Trento episode. As Schneider's Lenz advances towards his recovery, the Büchner model disappears from the text.

In a polemical assessment of the Büchner allusions, Peter Laemmle has rightly pointed out the tendency of newspaper reviewers to read Schneider's text in the light of the Büchner model, only to have sudden recourse to parallels with Goethe's *Italienische Reise* for the second half of the book.[6] What is striking from a detailed examination of the two texts is how inappropriate the Büchner model is, for although Schneider employs Büchner quotations to telling effect to convey Lenz's emotional crisis, he simultaneously limits their relevance by offering socio-political factors as an explanation for events. It is the oscillation between the psychological and the political, between the subjective and the objective, which is Schneider's concern throughout, a concern which critics have been slow to appreciate.[7] While the first sections portray a character struggling and failing to mediate between these possibilities, the end of the story brings successful mediation a step nearer. This interpretation may be illustrated with reference to another way in which the Büchner text serves as a model. Schneider's text is the more easily divided into sections because each section tends to begin with an adverb or adverbial phrase of time: 'morgens' (*L*, 5), 'an einem anderen Tag' (*L*, 8, 10, 14, 23) 'am nächsten Morgen' (*L*, 9), 'mitten in der Nacht' (*L*, 11), 'am Morgen um halb sieben' (*L*, 13), 'an einem Wochenende' (*L*, 16), 'am anderen Morgen' (*L*, 20, 51, 79), 'an einem Nachmittag' (*L*, 22, 31, 41), 'an einem Dienstag abend' (*L*, 27), 'An einem Samstag abend' (*L*, 37), 'ein paar Tage danach' (*L*, 46), 'am nächsten Tag' (*L*, 47), 'am Abend' (*L*, 50); 'nach einer Woche' (*L*, 56), 'ein paar Tage später' (*L*, 58, 90), 'nachts' (*L*, 64), 'später' (*L*, 70), 'eines Morgens' (*L*, 88), 'mittags' (*L*, 89). Again, it is significant that of the first twenty-five sections before Lenz leaves for Rome, nineteen begin thus, whereas only eight of the following eighteen sections do. The device is derived from Büchner's *Lenz*, bearing witness to the origins of that text in Oberlin's diary. While the adverbial phrases of time are not used explicitly to introduce sections, they are employed by Büchner to mark changes of mood. Schneider's decision to make far more striking and consistent use of the device in his narrative produces some unusual effects. It suggests that the narrative is, like Büchner's narrative, based on a diary, which establishes a claim to at least subjective authenticity for the experiences recorded; secondly, while appearing to offer a precise chronological framework, the narrative is effectively lifted out of history. Nowhere does Schneider give specific dates for events, even if it is possible from some internal events and from external evidence to locate the action between the spring and late summer of 1970. Time in Schneider's *Lenz* becomes pure succession, at least as far as the Berlin sections are concerned.[8] Lenz is portrayed as being temporarily trapped not only in his own subjectivity but also in his own time, though the reader is invited by the political debate which is part of the text to set this subjectivity in context, to supply a historical framework. Despite the dehistoricizing process, Schneider goes out of his way to place the action in a recognizable Berlin and to relate the subjective difficulties to objective problems, involving both the German past (located in Lenz's childhood) and the German present (the anti-Springer and anti-American demonstrations and the Maoist ideas of the early 1970s).[9] While Lenz's emotional crisis, his subjective self-absorption, tends to dehistoricize the action, Schneider is at pains to permit the reader to locate incidents in a specific historical, geographical and political situation, as if to supply a vantage-point outside Lenz's subjective experience.

If it is true that Lenz's initial difficulties, prompted by his break-up with L., involve his inability to mediate between his political insights and his emotional life, then it becomes important to examine his political views and their limitations. At the outset of the text, Lenz is viewed by the fellow members of the 'Betriebsgruppe' as a leading theorist, an author of many political pamphlets. The disagreement with Dieter is characteristic: Lenz cannot justify (or is unwilling to justify) his refusal to attend a demonstration. His explanation: 'ich träume zu schlecht' (*L*, 8), is sufficient explanation for Lenz, who is aware of the difficulty which he has in mediating between his emotional state and his political principles, but must strike Dieter as bizarre. Schneider is careful to alternate discursive scenes involving politics with practical involvement, either in the electronics factory where Lenz finds work or in demonstrations. These scenes deserve closer analysis, not least because Lenz becomes a more representative figure through his political activities and his awareness of their limitations.

One of the most illuminating (and funniest) scenes occurs in the seventeenth section, when Lenz attends a meeting of the 'Betriebsgruppe'. A Mao text is under discussion; the debate is predictable, complacent, politically correct. Isolated from the group by his emotional experiences, Lenz begins to reflect on the personal lives of the participants, on their psychological needs and drives, on their sexuality. Schneider juxtaposes Mao's text with Lenz's vision of spontaneous and violent action, in which the group members attack one another. The quotations employed are all taken from Mao's essay 'On Practice. On the Relation Between Knowledge and Practice, Between Knowing and Doing' (1937).[10] This was a seminal essay for the student movement and has direct relevance to Lenz's actions in Schneider's story, for, despite his awareness of the disparity between the revolutionary potentiality of the text and the bourgeois cosiness of the situation – 'Es kam ihm alles so artig, so nett vor' (*L*, 27) – he finds 'daß es gegen den Text gar nichts zu sagen gab' (*L*, 27). Mao's text, from which four quotations are supplied, offers an introduction to the dialectical relation between theory and practice; it is directed simultaneously against pragmatists who deny the values of theory and idealists who dismiss the usefulness of practice. Mao's conclusions offer, for the student generation depicted here, a programme for action: 'If you want knowledge, you must take part in the practice of changing reality . . . If you want to know the theory and methods of revolution, you must take part in revolution.'[11]

Much of Schneider's *Lenz* consists of attempts by Lenz to translate the theory of revolution into practice, and at the same time to correct his original theories by reference back to his actual experiences, in other words to test out the dialectical nature of knowing and doing. When Lenz attends an interview for the job in the electronics factory, he is clearly given precedence over the foreigners, Greeks and Turks, who are seeking work. Out of a mixture of guilt and curiosity, Lenz befriends one of the Turks: 'er hatte den heftigen Wunsch, die Welt durch seine Augen zu sehen' (*L*, 11). Although he grasps in theory the situation of exploitation and the sense of vulnerability of the Turkish *Gastarbeiter*, he seeks

to know what it feels like. The irony is that his efforts to experience
the world of work, to view society from below, effectively debar a
needy 'Gastarbeiter' from obtaining employment; although he is
unaware of it, it is likely that Lenz actively contributes to the
Turk's eventual deportation. The constant threat of deportation is
a motif which will recur in the text: Lenz's friend Walter has been
deported from Spain for making disparaging remarks about Franco
(*L*, 14) and is in the privileged position of knowing what it feels
like; only at the end of the novel, when Lenz himself is deported
from Italy, will he be able to step into the shoes of the dispos-
sessed. The motif of wearing someone else's clothes signals
throughout the possibility of experiencing from the inside the
situation of another. Examples abound: Lenz and Walter exchange
clothes during the shoe-buying episode (Section 10); Lenz reflects
that L. had made all the important decisions about his clothes,
defining for him an identity with which he had been content
(Section 21); in Rome, he attends a party in an ill-fitting borrowed
suit, signalling his sense of unease with this alien identity (Section
34); and finally, in Trento, he immerses himself in the life of
another community, symbolized by his acquisition of cast-off
clothes from his new Italian friends. Clothes, then, mark more or
less successful attempts at stepping into the lives of others, at
experiencing the psychological truth of what is a theoretical,
political insight.

Revolutionary action, frequently depicted through the motif of
stone-throwing, serves as a further illustration of the same point.
During the demonstration at the Greek embassy and the *Amerika-
haus*, Lenz listens sympathetically to the account of a younger
colleague of his first experience of stone-throwing:

> Er beschrieb ihm genau, wie er mit dem Stein in der Hand vor dem
> Amerikahaus stand, den Arm erst so locker hin und her schlenkerte, als
> wäre kein Stein darin, den Stein beim Anblick eines Passanten er-
> schrocken fallen ließ, wie er ihn dann mit einer heftigen Wut, er wußte
> nicht, ob es die Wut über seine Unentschlossenheit oder über die
> Amerikaner war, wieder aufhob und in die Fensterscheibe schleuderte.
> Hinterher habe er sich so frei gefühlt wie noch nie, er könne gar nicht
> beschreiben, was für ein Gefühl das sei. (*L*, 24)

Lenz recalls his own similar experience, and although he has
come to realize that the political relevance of a demonstration has
little enough to do with the psychology of overcoming one's

personal fear of violent action, he wonders whether his new theoretical understanding has merely resulted in the loss of spontaneous anger. In the following episode, Lenz takes up the question of stone-throwing in his debate with his patron, who, while welcoming the impetus which the student rebellion has given to the democratic process, has always warned of the dangers of violence. Although Lenz has come to the same conclusions, he distances himself emphatically from his patron: 'Es ist aber nicht das gleiche, wenn einer, der statt des Kugelschreibers nie einen Stein in die Hand nahm, jetzt das Werfen von Steinen verurteilt mit den gleichen Sätzen, mit denen ein anderer die Erfahrung beschreibt, daß es sinnlos geworden ist, Steine zu werfen' (*L*, 26). Lenz's position is a Maoist one: his theoretical insight has been gained in and through practical involvement; it is thus of a different order of truth from the purely theoretical position of his patron. Lenz's debate with his patron permits Schneider to indulge in some topical sparring with Günter Grass, whose *örtlich betäubt* (1969) similarly explores the problematic nature of direct action and the psychological mechanisms which underlie political protest.[12] For Lenz, stone-throwing for political purposes is replaced by stone-throwing out of psychological necessity, either in shattering the image of the city reflected in the canal water, or in dropping flowerpots on to cars parked below the Rome apartment where the party is held, to signal his childish irritation with the radical *chic* of Roman intellectuals. The functional shift in this single motif from the socio-political (Berlin) to the psychological (Rome) echoes the structure of the story as a whole.

Lenz's political difficulties are exacerbated, rather than resolved, by his attempts to experience proletarian working conditions in the factory. In the first place, he is privileged by being offered work at all; secondly, it is assumed that he is skilled, and repetitive work on the assembly line is given to him only grudgingly, at his insistence. Although Lenz is himself unaware of the contradictions in his behaviour (and the narrative perspective which vouchsafes to the reader only Lenz's inner experience reinforces this impression) his behaviour appears both misguided and self-indulgent. While he is seeking earnestly to improve the lot of the oppressed workers, he manages only to make it more likely that the Turkish worker will be deported. Far from breaking down the barrier between theory and practice, he actually reinforces it. The novelty of the repetitive work swiftly wears off; Lenz's irritation at the

oppressive conditions is matched by his sense of isolation, his sense
of being observed by others. He is capable of articulating the
workers' complaints, of expounding the theory of late capitalism,
but precisely this ability distances him from the mainly female
workforce: 'Ihm war, als könne er was gut machen, eine
unbekannte Schuld abtragen' (*L*, 22).

His guilt feelings are complex: his desire to identify emotionally
with the oppressed is vitiated by his equally powerful urge to
preach the gospel of Mao to the uninitiated. Yet the guilt is also
personal: his relationship to L. was, in Maoist terms, an attempt to
bridge the gap between knowing and doing. He admits, at least to
himself, that L. embodied the harmony of essence and appearance,
of theory and practice. That he has not bought any clothes since L.
left, since she chose suitable things for him, signals (again through
the dressing-up motif) that she had given him an identity with
which he was content, but which has now proved unreliable. The
language of politics is used to explain the impossibility of their
relationship: L., a working-class girl, sought through him a
theoretical understanding of her position, a security and reassur-
ance; he sought through her access to a directly experienced,
spontaneous world. Their relationship is doomed because she
acquires through him bourgeois aspirations (which he despises)
and he through her a proletarian directness (which she abhors).
Having awakened his sensuality, she vehemently objects to his
attempts to experiment with that sensuality. Lenz's practical
attempt to bridge the class divide, to transcend, through love, the
clash between theory and practice, proves to be a failure.

The discrepancy between knowing and doing, between theory
and some of the botched attempts to translate it into practice, is the
source of a number of humorous scenes in *Lenz*, the comic nature
of which critics have hitherto been reluctant to acknowledge. Henri
Bergson's *Le Rire*, with its classic definition of laughter as the
corrective which life applies to the rigid and inflexible, offers an
appropriate model. Knowing, when knowledge degenerates into
theoretical inflexibility, can be deflated by confronting it with
doing, where action appears at once both to be the logical outcome
of theory and ludicrously at odds with it. Significantly, it is at the
parties, both in Berlin and Rome, that the discrepancy between
theory and practice is presented as social comedy. Lenz's response
to the questions posed by the critic (Neidt) about his current
activities is to embark on a pantomime, taking up the implications

of the critic's statements, his language and gestures, and exaggerating them:

> Wenn der Blick des Kritikers bei dem Wort Arbeiterklasse an Lenz vorbei in die Ferne schweifte, deutete Lenz mit dem Arm in die Blickrichtung des Kritikers, als liefe die Arbeiterklasse dort gerade vorbei. Blitzte bei dem Wort Opportunist Haß in dem Auge des Kritikers auf, dann ballte Lenz bestätigend die Faust. Schließlich waren beide soweit, daß sie im Chor dem Opportunismus und allen Spielarten den Krieg erklärten. Sofort sah sich Lenz nach einem Gegenstand um, an dem sie ein Exempel statuieren könnten. Lenz deutete auf die Bücherwand, die bis unter die Decke mit opportunistischen Schriftstellern gefüllt war. Er riß einige Bände von Goethe aus dem Regal, forderte den Kritiker auf, bei einer Jugendstilvase mit anzufassen und deutete auf ein Bild an der Wand, das Che Guevara als leidenden Christus darstellte. Der Kritiker war entsetzt. (*L*, 39)

The contrast between the designer *chic* and the proletarian sympathies of the Roman intellectuals is presented in similarly comic fashion. Lenz's encounter with the famous writer, his patron (Section 16), culminates in the latter's offer to help Lenz involve himself in more practical political activity. This work appears to have something to do with the European Community and the butter mountain, for as the writer outlines his position, Lenz is left with the vision of the writer 'mit einem Spaten vor einem riesigen Butterberg stehen' (*L*, 26), a vision which vividly captures the comic potentialities of the discrepancy between political theory and its practical realization. Apart from its comic potential, the way in which his Berlin colleagues define identity in terms of political activism is reflected in casual conversation: the initial question posed by his acquaintances is almost exclusively directed towards what he has been *doing*, or, at the very least, what he plans to do. Dieter raises the question of participation in the demonstration; Marina, even as a prelude to their sexual encounter, 'stellte dann das übliche Verhör mit ihm an, was er mache, in welcher Gruppe er arbeite' (*L*, 9); the critic at the party first wants to know 'was Lenz mache' (*L*, 38) and finally 'worauf er hinauswolle, welches Ziel er verfolge' (*L*, 40); B. 'fragte Lenz, was er mache' (*L*, 48). Pierra, by contrast, 'stellte Lenz keine Fragen, was er in den letzten drei Jahren gemacht habe' (*L*, 62).

A further example of Lenz's difficulties with politics is represented in his ambivalence towards cars. In theory, at least, cars are a potent symbol of West German consumer fetishism: Lenz is struck by the fact that minor alterations in the styling of Volkswagen cars are as fascinating to consumers as are major changes in the political situation to him and his friends (Section 18). The significance of this excursus on consumerism becomes clear from Schneider's essay 'Die Phantasie im Spätkapitalismus und die Kulturrevolution'. Here he distinguishes the 'Gebrauchswert' of a car, the functional value attaching to a means of transport, from its 'Tauschwert', the value it acquires in the market strategies of late capitalism. To the embarrassment of the Left, Brecht loved cars; yet what might appear to be an aberration can be explained away. Brecht's enthusiasm was confined to the car as a means of transport; he experienced the car in the 1920s as a new productive force and could hence employ it as a poetic image. Only in late capitalism has the emphasis shifted, Schneider argues, from the productive value of cars to their marketability. Minor changes in models have no functional value and merely serve to stimulate sales: 'Beispiel VW. Der VW war Mitte des Jahrhunderts fertig und brauchbar. Weiterzuentwickeln war von nun an nicht der VW, sondern die Fähigkeit des Menschen, ihn zu gebrauchen' (*AP*, 150). Schneider's analysis explains why Lenz can be at once dismissive of the window-shoppers who stare at the latest VW model, or drop flowerpots on the status symbols of the Roman communist *chic*, and enjoy the sensation of speed as he drives with B. along the *autostrada* from Rome to Trento. As the car in which they are travelling regains its functional value, as its speed alters Lenz's perceptions, offering him 'das richtige Tempo für meine Wahrnehmungen' (*L*, 75), it lays claim once again to the poetic quality which it had for Brecht. The rejection of consumer fetishism was, of course, a constituent feature of the student movement; this explains why, when Lenz looks in a shop window, it is merely to flirt with a shop assistant; and why Lenz is permitted to engage in casual shoplifting.

If the political, social and historical explanations are paramount in Berlin, Lenz's carefully planned and obviously temporary flight to Rome (the rent on his Berlin flat having been paid for two months in advance) offers him an excess of psychological explanations. The actress Pierra, with whom he takes up a desultory relationship, is a reader of palms: 'Sie erklärte ihm, daß die linke Handhälfte die nach außen gerichteten Energien des Menschen ausdrücken, während die rechte die Kräfte zeigt, die im Unbewußten wirken, daß die wichtigsten Linien schon bei der Geburt ausgeprägt sind und mit dem Tod aus der Handfläche verschwinden' (*L*, 63). Lenz is struck by the capacity of Roman intellectuals to seek hidden meanings behind the slightest gesture: 'Sie interessierten sich nicht für gesellschaftliche Vorgänge, aber für ihre Träume fühlten sie sich verantwortlich' (*L*, 70). The over-emphasis on the psychological, the obsession with hidden motives and inner needs, answer at one level Lenz's earlier puzzlement. In Berlin his reaction to dreams had been one of irritation, of uncertainty; he had questioned the inner, subjective needs of his fellow members of the 'Betriebs-gruppe', but had found his insights subversive of a sense of community and solidarity. In Rome, he feels no such qualms, for inauthenticity of behaviour is ubiquitous. The salon communists at the Roman party feel no compulsion to mean what they say, or dress in accordance with recognizable norms. Signs and their significance point in opposite directions: 'Immer, wenn Lenz auf das hörte, was gesagt wurde, verstand er die Gesten nicht, die die Reden begleiteten, achtete er auf die Gesten, so verstand er nicht, was gesagt wurde' (*L*, 68). Pierra seems to live in the present more intensely than any German, partly, he surmises, because she is constantly aware of the past, surrounded by monuments which recall both a cultural and a personal history for her. Lenz is struck by the contrast with Germany, where 'in geschichtslosen Städten' (*L*, 69) it is difficult to live intensely in the present; perhaps it is 'dieses angstlose Zusammenleben mit der Vergangenheit' which enables one 'sich in der Gegenwart einzurichten' (*L*, 69–70). The Roman experience proves to be a decisive stage in Lenz's develop-ment, for it supplies a powerful antidote to his over-reliance on political theory. Moreover, it is during his encounter with Pierra that he begins to confront uncomfortable personal memories from his childhood. He embarks, as it were, on an 'angstloses Zusam-menleben mit der Vergangenheit'.

The Berlin sections of the text offer only one childhood memory, triggered by the smell of the chestnut blossom, while the Roman episode suddenly prompts a series of intensely vivid and personal recollections. His sexual encounter with Pierra conjures up a series of images from his past life reminiscent of the Fellini allusions in the opening section of the text: 'Alte, versunkene Bilder tauchten wieder auf' (*L*, 63). The process of remembering operates in reverse: recent recollections of his life with L. are superseded by childhood experiences, juvenile fits of rage directed against authority figures:

'er beschimpfte seinen Vater, seinen Lehrer, den Kritiker' (*L*, 63). Lenz's rebelliousness, defined in the Berlin sections as an expression of political outrage, is here reinterpreted in psychological terms. In the following section, when the train to Ostia suddenly stops in open country, Lenz recalls a wartime experience, when, with his mother on a train attacked by an enemy plane, most passengers flee to the woods, only to return when the attack is over. Lenz, who mentions his mother for the first time in the text at this point, interprets his subsequent instability, his restlessness, as a product of this formative experience. Whether it is represented as an authoritarian father-figure or as a vulnerable mother-figure, the German past is vividly reconstituted. While Pierra's reaction is to recommend a good analyst, the reader is left in little doubt that the access which Lenz gains to his childhood is part of the process of recovery from his crisis. Yet it is only later, in Trento, when he begins to integrate himself into the life of the community, that he is able to confront the full implications of his memories, dreams and reflections. In the thirty-ninth section his newly acquired confidence in himself permits the most frank confessions: he sees his mother walking in the mountains with a man who is not his father: 'Er spürte eine unerträgliche Angst, daß seine Mutter ihn mit diesem fremden Mann verließ' (*L*, 85). Then he recalls, as an eight-year-old, staying out at night, returning in the early hours, and being severely punished by his mother, who left the following morning to visit his father, who was staying in another town, and who died there. It is as if his relationships with other women, in particular with L., involved a re-creation of this crucial experience: namely, to disobey and wound, to force L., as a surrogate for his mother, to suffer 'als wollte er beweisen, daß es ihm nichts ausmachte, der Mörder seiner Mutter zu sein' (*L*, 85). Lenz's integration into the community in Trento is made possible, not least, because he is able to take the first tentative steps towards an understanding of his own personal anxiety and guilt. Trento clearly offers him other compensations: he is accepted for what he is; he delights in his capacity to slip into a new identity, to combine his theoretical insights with new practical involvement. Yet it is his growth in self-awareness, his acceptance of his personal past, which is a key to his new maturity. In accepting the past, he is capable of experiencing the present more intensely. Although he is finally deported from Italy by an outside agency, he has already accepted the necessity for leaving. He has realized that his attempt to assume another identity is at best escapist, at worst counter-productive. The clothes which he has donned do not belong to him: 'Plötzlich war ihm, als säße er neben sich und sähe sich da sitzen' (*L*, 89). That he is deported as a German, that he has come to accept his own problematic personal identity, signals the start of his recovery.

The structural parallels between the Berlin and the Roman episodes are a feature of Schneider's text. Each location offers a series of encounters, a series of incidents, which parallel those of the other setting: the unsatisfactory relationship with Marina is echoed by the equally unsatisfactory relationship with Pierra; the Berlin party offers Lenz insight into the self-deception of German intellectuals, while the Roman party offers precisely the same insights into the contradictions of the Italian Left. Both the incident at the canal in Berlin (Section 12) and that on the beach near Rome (Section 30) offer momentary release in the contemplation of water. While the emphasis of the Berlin sections lies on political analysis, this is found to be insufficient to account for his personal grief at the loss of L. The Roman sections offer an antidote, a reinterpretation of Lenz's actions and reactions as dictated entirely by individual psychology. Only when he has undergone this therapy is he able, in Trento, to mediate successfully between these equally convincing, but, in isolation, equally inadequate explanations.

The Trento scenes, apart from offering invaluable access to personal memory, also provide Lenz with a broader perspective, signalled by the vantage-point of the mountain-top, high above the town. Looking down on the town, Lenz is struck first by the stillness: 'Kein Geräusch, keine Bewegung, in dem Licht stand alles ruhig und fest da, die Ruhe machte Lenz keine Angst' (*L*, 79). His aesthetic delight in the landscape gives way to a socio-political interpretation of the scene as a setting for the class struggle. What follows is tantamount to a conversion: 'Wie er da oben stand und hinunterschaute, erschienen ihm die Kämpfe, die er auf dem Schauplatz seiner Seele austrug, unwichtig und lächerlich. Er spürte, wie sich die Richtung seiner Aufmerksamkeit änderte, wie seine Augen aufhörten, nach innen zu schauen. Er mochte nicht mehr da oben bleiben, er wollte hinunter . . .' (*L*, 80–1). The distance, the panorama, has permitted Lenz a broader perspective on his situation. The tension between knowing and doing which had lent his political commitment such a tragi-comic air in Berlin, the obsessive psychologizing in Rome which had thrown him back

on his own subjectivity, these are now resolved in a new understanding of his relationship to society. His behaviour now becomes
spontaneous, no longer conditioned by theoretical considerations;
a new sensitivity to sensuous experience is manifest: he begins to
take an interest in food and in imaginative literature, both of which
had seemed suspect to him in Berlin. His reawakening does not
betoken an abandonment of politics; it is simply that knowing and
doing, that theory and practice, no longer point in opposite
directions.

The final section of the text, presenting Lenz's return to Berlin,
repays closer analysis. Lenz, who has now recovered from his
crisis, initially perceives little change; everything has continued as
it was, yet radical changes have taken place in the lives of his
acquaintances. It is, in fact, Lenz's dual and simultaneous perception of stasis and change which indicates the progress which he has
made. He is, thanks to his experiences, sensitive both to the
continuities born of individual psychology and the discontinuities
prompted by historical change. Alive to his own personal memories, he is also able to place them in context, to see them as having
shaped his values and expectations. The much analysed 'Dableiben'
with which the book closes, is, on this score, a positive decision.[13]
It betokens assent to his own identity in a specific place; it reflects
his understanding of his own past; and is, in however tentative a
form, a vote of confidence in his German identity.

Notes

[1] See Rolf Hosfeld and Helmut Peitsch, '"Weil uns diese Aktionen
innerlich verändern, sind sie politisch". Bemerkungen zu vier Romanen
über die Studentenbewegung', *Basis. Jahrbuch für deutsche
Gegenwartsliteratur*, 8 (1978), 92–114, and Malcolm Pender, 'Historical
awareness and Peter Schneider's *Lenz*', *German Life and Letters*, 37 No. 2
(January 1984), 150–60.
[2] Georg Büchner, *Sämtliche Werke und Briefe*, Historisch-kritische
Ausgabe, ed. Werner R. Lehmann (Hamburg, Christian Wegner Verlag,
1967), I, 80, ll. 17–18 and 22–3.
[3] Ibid., I, 80, ll. 13–15.
[4] Ibid., I, 82, ll. 29–30; ll. 36–7; l. 39.
[5] Ibid., I, 89–90, ll. 38–9 and 1–2.
[6] Peter Laemmle, 'Büchners Schatten. Kritische Überlegungen zur
Rezeption von Peter Schneiders Erzählung *Lenz*', *Akzente* (1974), 469–78.

[7] A striking exception is Peter Labanyi, 'When Wishing Still Helped: Peter Schneider's Left-Wing Melancholy', in *After the Death of Literature: West German Writing of the 1970s*, ed. Keith Bullivant (Oxford, Providence, Munich, Berg, 1989), 313–39. Labanyi, in the course of his illuminating essay on Schneider, is right to argue that 'the media stereotype of a "turn" from politics to subjectivity . . . needs to be relativised by an insistence – exemplified within the Student Movement – that the personal *is* the political' (313).

[8] Rolf Hosfeld and Helmut Peitsch (see note 3) are right both to highlight this 'Ent-historisierungstechnik' and to point to its origins in Büchner's *Lenz*.

[9] Michael Buselmeier, 'Peter Schneider', in *Kritisches Lexikon zur deutschsprachigen Gegenwartsliteratur*, ed. Heinz Ludwig Arnold, notes that Schneider avoids historical detail, but immediately adds: 'Aufgrund von Indizien kann man als Haupthandlungsort Westberlin, als Zeitspanne Frühjahr bis Herbst 1969 erschließen' (2).

[10] Mao Tse-Tung, *Four Essays on Philosophy* (Peking, Foreign Languages Press, 1966), 1–22.

[11] Ibid., 8. This quotation follows immediately after the lines quoted by Schneider, 29.

[12] The central metaphor in Grass's *örtlich betäubt* may well have inspired Schneider to employ the topos of teeth, though the allusion in *Lenz* is to Polanski's film *Dance of the Vampires*. Wolfgang, the young worker, projects on to the members of the 'Betriebsgruppe' his own sense of alienation from their theoretical intellectualizing about society. His working-class origins mark him out as different from the group; they are the vampires intent on sucking his blood.

[13] Keith Bullivant, *Realism Today: Aspects of the Contemporary West German Novel* (Leamington Spa, Berg, 1987), puts forward both interpretations simultaneously: 'He returns to Berlin, and although nothing seems to have changed in his absence, he is filled with new-found energy . . . The "cured" Lenz has a clear purpose: "Dableiben". Although it would not be wrong to allow for a different reading of the final scene – with the "Dableiben" seen as Lenz's self-deception about his immediate future – Schneider . . . shrinks from following through and showing us the results of Lenz's change' (112).

6

Defending an Exemplary Failure:
On the Paradoxical Unity of *Atempause,*
Die Wette and Other Works by Peter Schneider

R. M. GILLETT

Peter Schneider's first book opens with the words: 'Wir haben Fehler gemacht' (*AN,* 7). In the early essay reprinted at the start of *Atempause* the 'Mängel' are those of the 'gegenwärtige Literaturkritik'.[1] In the 'Nachwort' to that book, the failings are in the first person.[2] The attack on the critics is brilliant. In it Schneider groups together five influential arbiters of taste in various ways so as to expose the subterfuges they adopt and the weaknesses of their style. The closing re-evaluation is anything but brilliant. There is a clumsiness about it which extends even to the author's telling us what he can see from his window at the time of writing (*AP,* 208). In the earlier diatribe there is no window, no time, almost no author. Instead there is the odd rhetorical *pointe* which seems to belong to the world of the public prosecutor.[3] Although the ostensible subject of the reviews reviewed is a novel by Max Frisch, Schneider's own opinion of that text is carefully excluded. In the postface then, Schneider specifically and deliberately sets out to make good such omissions. By detailing the emotions of a young political speech-writer, for example, he rescues rhetoric from anonymity.[4] He excuses what is to my mind one of the most unreadable pieces in the book and to his one of the most paradoxically dated on the grounds that it is rooted in personal despair (*AP,* 210). And he atones for his reductive treatment of Weiss's *Marat-Sade* by documenting his passionate reactions to the play and to a reading by Weiss himself (*AP,* 217f.).

In other words, the final item of *Atempause* is not only not brilliant; it is actively seeking to eschew brilliance. In it, the whole view of life which takes brilliance as a criterion is represented by Barbara. Originally the centre of a rather demanding coterie of bright young things, she is abandoned first by her Greek boyfriend and then by an increasing number of newly activist students. Finally her stress on brilliance becomes an alibi for whole-scale defection: because her literal espousal of American ideals extends to actively supporting subversive intervention in Greek affairs, it can clearly be read as an act of revenge for the slights of the Berlin years. When she then describes Schneider as the opposite of brilliant, as 'provinziell', he takes that as a compliment. But his triumph is mitigated by sadness because he is aware of the loneliness and bad faith informing that judgement (*AP*, 213–15).

Part of the strategy for eschewing brilliance, therefore, is precisely to emphasize loneliness in order to undercut bad faith. That is why Schneider is concerned in the afterword to reinsert the writing self into the text. The gaze out of the Berlin window is an extension of the vision of a tramp's sleeping place, and a direct result of it (*AP*, 217–18). For if there be traces of them that have left empty bottles and old newspapers behind, how much more should there be of those who have left articles and collections of essays. Hence the shock Schneider feels when he discovers that the only trace his subjective experience has left on his early works is the illusion of objectivity.

The creation of such an illusion, of course, was precisely the purpose of the subterfuges attacked by Schneider in the opening essay of *Atempause*. To counter it, he will insist on the element of personal commitment. He knows that looking to literature to be the exclusive provider of ideals is asking too much (*AP*, 215). So he asks that it should at least be honest in declaring its own standpoint (*AP*, 30). The whole of *Atempause* is carefully structured so as to illustrate this position. An early article on Westerns, for example, couched in the language of the university seminar, is countered and corrected by Schneider's curiously naïve account of his later attempt to explain what it was about an amateur film that had moved him.[5] The first set of reviews, in which enthusiasm, unease and maybe even jealousy are hidden or denied by the use of the third person singular, is answered by the second set, where the personal response of the writer to his subject is deliberately foregrounded. Where the outer edges of the symmetry set clarity against loss of clarity, brilliance against provincialism, objectivity against subjectivity, dispassionate rhetoric against commitment, so the centre is provided by that essay in which an extreme of personal anguish, loneliness, loss of love and intellectual uncertainty is expressed in a plethora of Marxist vocabulary.[6] On either side of

it stand a nit-picking, 'academic' essay on the political inefficacity
of Brecht's *Arturo Ui* and the warm, witty, direct lecture-text on
the 'Unterschied von Literatur und Politik'.[7]

Thus it is in the book's construction that its message and its
significance is to be found, and with it the justification for reprint-
ing old pieces. In this sense the subtitle, which defines the book as
a 'Versuch . . . zu ordnen', is to be taken literally and seriously.
Nor is the arguably awkward use of the possessive adjective in it
('*meine* Gedanken') accidental or incompetent. And the quotation
printed on the cover would also seem to have been carefully
chosen to underline the book's dialectic purpose:

> Allerdings! Ich reiße Zitate aus ihrem Zusammenhang. Was ich be-
> schimpfe, das beschreibe ich unvollständig, und ich denke nicht daran,
> mich auf gewisse Voraussetzungen einzulassen. Mit einem Wort: ich
> bin einseitig. Aber das hindert mich nicht daran, recht zu haben. (*AP*,
> 87)

Taken on its own, as its epigraphic character encourages us to
do, this quotation can indeed be read, as Gordon Burgess reads it,
as a 'defiantly' provocative remark'.[8] Coming as it does from a
known adherent of student revolt, it can be seen as a categorical
refusal to keep to the rules of well-mannered literary critical discourse. It can even be interpreted as a declaration of intent to
plagiarize with malice aforethought. In its immediate context,
however, it takes on a very different set of overtones. There, in the
article of 1966 about 'Happenings', 'Fluxus' and 'Pop Art', it is
tantamount to an act of pre-emptive strategic defence. It is
designed to defuse the argument that anybody who attacks pop
art necessarily does so on the basis of inadequate engagement
with it. Thus by insisting on his right to adopt a partial point of
view, Schneider is paradoxically defending his impartiality. For
this reason it is perfectly logical that the essay which begins with
these words should belong to the first half of the book. For the
self in it is in point of fact a mere non-committal subterfuge.

At the same time, of course, because the book later acknow-
ledges and rejects the bad faith of that subterfuge, the quotation
on its cover necessarily takes on yet another meaning. It can
indeed be read as an attack on the abstractions of the New Criticism. But the suggested alternative is no longer political upheaval
or orthodox Marxism. It is openness to enjoyment – jargonizable

as culinary individualism. Now it is almost a platitude that the tide of revolution subsumes the self for a while and then strands it again. So when in his epigraph Schneider reinvests his words with his own personality, he is transposing them into an aftermath. The atmosphere of that aftermath pervades the whole of Schneider's writing. And the effect is to make of it, from the very beginning, a literature of exemplary failure: 'wir haben Fehler gemacht'.

Perhaps it is not surprising that literary critics, who, as Schneider himself has shown, are better prepared by both temperament and training to respond to brilliance than to personality, should be more adept at pointing up what they consider to be Schneider's literary failures than at exploring the implications of this literature of failure. And there can be no doubt at all but that Schneider is playing an extremely dangerous game. For it is very hard to invest subjective responses to art with any kind of transitive validity. Furthermore, there is the constant danger of succumbing to the mimetic fallacy. As Schneider himself puts it: 'Ein Stotterer ist nicht der geeignete Mann, um einen Stotterer darzustellen' (*AP*, 103). And an admission of weakness, especially if it is expressed in terms of paradox or contradiction, can easily have the effect not of disarming opponents, but of arming them.

Thus it is noticeable that a considerable proportion of the secondary material I have read on Schneider operates with precisely those distinctions which structure the symmetry of *Atempause* and are therefore called into question by it.[9] Take for example Michael Buselmeier's criticism of *Lenz*.[10] It may of course be simply in the service of information that he supplies the sales figures for the story – though the tone and the terms in which he seeks an explanation would suggest otherwise. Nor is there anything automatically exceptionable about the statement that: 'Nun haben aber Brüche in der politischen Biographie eines Menschen Brüche in dessen innerer Biographie zur Folge (und umgekehrt)' (Buselmeier, 2). But the conclusion he goes on to draw from this is symptomatically tendentious and untenable: 'Es ist nicht unangemessen, wenn ein Leser von der halbautobiographischen Erzählung eines politischen Autors mehr erwartet als die aktuelle Beschreibung innerer Schwierigkeiten' (ibid.).

Clearly the double negative here in itself already points the way to and invites a first rebuff. For any response which refuses to take a text on its own terms but applies to it spurious expectations derived from elsewhere is indeed 'unangemessen'. Fortunately, this attitude is only rarely to be met with in ordinary readers – it is rather a besetting sin of the critic. Then the term 'halbautobiographisch', though to my mind it is semi-meaningless in the context, does refer to a persistent distinction which Schneider in *Atempause* refuses to recognize. For if the final essay of that collection deals with views from various Berlin windows, that is because it enshrines the awareness that *all* writing, even sentences which ultimately find their way into the speeches of unknown politicians, is up to a point profoundly autobiographical. (That the story *Lenz* does not go beyond that point is made clear by Schneider's 'response to an anonymous critic' which is importantly reprinted in *Atempause*.[11]) By the same token, of course, and to the same extent, all reading is also autobiographical. And it is precisely to these twin insights, which, as we have seen, are both stressed in *Atempause*, that the story *Lenz* owes its existence.

The suggestion that the author of that story is a 'politischer Autor' is also problematical – not least because it blurs precisely the distinction which Schneider was so concerned to draw at the heart of *Atempause*. It is perfectly true that where Büchner's Lenz was primarily assailed by metaphysical or theological problems, Schneider not infrequently adds or substitutes political ones. But that no more makes Schneider a political author than it makes Büchner a theologian. It is generally acknowledged that one author of *Lenz* was politically active during the student revolt of the late 1960s – though at the time, of course, he was not yet the author of his *Lenz*. Indeed, he couldn't be, because he was too busy being political to be an author. Nor is there any denying that Peter Schneider has written extensively on matters bearing directly or indirectly on issues which could be described as 'political' (though even here the line is not an easy one to draw). But none the less to describe him as a 'political author' is to ascribe to him and to his texts an overt tendency which they simply do not have. In this sense there is a valid distinction to be made between a politician who writes, a propagandist, and a writer who happens to number politics among his themes. It is a distinction exemplified in *Atempause* by the twin figures of Lenin and Gorki. And it seems clear that Schneider aligns himself with Gorki rather than with Lenin.

The phrase 'die aktuelle Beschreibung innerer Schwierigkeiten' is particularly revealing. As a characterization of *Vati* it might be hard to better. As a summary of all there is to *Lenz*, however, it is simple hypallage. There the vehicle for the transmission of intellectual and emotional uncertainties, so far from being 'aktuell' is doubly historical. If anything, the difficulties themselves can be seen as rooted in the immediate past and therefore 'aktuell'. In which case, of course, the exclusive epithet of inwardness would necessarily cease to apply. Here too it is possible to detect the operation of antinomies undermined by *Atempause*. For in his apology for the pivotal essay of that book, Schneider presents it precisely as the 'aktuelle Beschreibung innerer Schwierigkeiten'. His insistence that the seemingly timeless generalities of 'Die Phantasie im Spätkapitalismus und die Kulturrevolution' are, in their very seeming timelessness and generality, inextricably bound up with the political events of the time in which they were written and hence datedly specific, necessarily calls into question the whole concept of 'Aktualität'. And the revelation that the apparently objective argument may well have been motivated by the turmoil in the author's personal life indicates that the distinction between inner and outer difficulties is not one which can meaningfully be drawn with regard to works of literature.

Taken together, Buselmeier's specious antinomies can be seen as adumbrating three charges regularly, though not always explicitly, levelled against Schneider. The first is two-pronged. It begins, as Buselmeier does, with the accusation that Schneider's protagonists are merely thinly-veiled self-portraits and goes on to expose the use of newspaper reports and other documentary material. In other, more drastic, words, the progression is from monomania, via paucity of invention, to plagiarism. Nor is it of any avail to suggest that the first and third of these terms ought by rights to cancel each other out. Once the second has stuck, it can be used to explain even mutually contradictory strategies of concealment.

Now it was the charge of plagiarism, of course, which fuelled the controversy surrounding *Vati*.[12] And Gordon Burgess subtly returns to it in his article.[13] There he is concerned to draw yet a further distinction, between 'journalism' on the one hand and 'literature' on the other. He notes the sheer statistical preponderance of the former over the latter in Schneider's work and suggests that it may have had a deleterious effect on his creative writing. Since he goes on to show how in . . . *schon bist du ein Verfassungsfeind* Schneider is 'successfully reworking authentic material into a literary artefact' (110) and to insist that 'what does

distinguish *Der Mauerspringer* . . . is the overridingly imaginative
use which Schneider has made of his material' (111), it is hard not
to conclude that the perceived failure of *Vati* must be put down to
inappropriate subject-matter and bad workmanship rather than to
the application of an erroneous principle.

And indeed, it seems to me that it is important to note the
extent to which Schneider's 'journalism' and his 'literature' re-
inforce each other. Thus the section of *Lenz* which is set in 'einer
Elektrofirma' is clearly related to Schneider's *Kursbuch* article on
'Die Frauen bei Bosch'.[14] Similarly the article on the 'Berliner
Volksschule' not only breathes the same atmosphere as the 'Lehrer
Kleff', but also, in the compassionate depiction of the divided
classroom, characteristically uses realistic detail to illuminate both
social alienation and the essence of the schizophrenic city.[15]
Equally, the beginning of *Der Mauerspringer* could appear in *Freibeuter* without either altering the nature of that publication or
being untrue to itself.[16] So when in Heinz Ludwig Arnold's *Bestandsaufnahme Gegenwartsliteratur* Schneider makes a plea for an
'essayistischen Roman', he can again be seen to be urging the
abandonment of untenable antitheses which critics none the less
feel justified in using against him.[17]

Whether *Vati* can rightly be described as an 'essayistische Erzählung' is a moot point. Burgess's view, at all events, is that in
taking material from *Bunte* and elsewhere and putting it into a
work of literature, Schneider is depriving it of the effectiveness it
gained from its original context without attempting to restore that
effectiveness by other means appropriate to the new context. It is
a view rooted in the belief that the story of Josef and Rolf Mengele can legitimately be sensationalized. Again and again what
Burgess objects to in Schneider's use of his material is the loss of
that heightened impact which in his view makes for good journalism. When he then goes on hypothetically to quote Eagleton to the
effect that this intensification of ordinary language is a distin-
guishing feature of literature, this not only collapses his original
distinction – it also, more worryingly, has the effect of claiming
the accolade of literature for the letters of Josef Mengele. Viewed
from this perspective, it is at least understandable, and perhaps
not wholly blameworthy, that Schneider should wish to align
what he writes with a somewhat different conception of literature.
Hence where Burgess sees in Mengele's use of nouns the attribute
of a written style which has 'the concentrated quality of distilled

thought', Schneider draws attention to the same, surely suspect, phenomenon by encapsulating the reaction of the generation of the sons and daughters in a weary gesture of dismissal: '"Ach Vati, deine Substantive!"'.[18]

There is absolutely no doubt but that Burgess is right to qualify this passage as 'bathos' (Burgess, 118). It is of a piece with his quoted view of literature, too, that he should use the word more in the sense of a general objurgation than as a technical term of formal rhetoric. But it is still slightly surprising, in the light of the obtrusive water-pump and the narratorial signpost, that he should never for one moment explore the possibility that this may be deliberate. Even when he is reading the essay from *Deutsche Ängste* where this possibility is presented as a fact, Burgess assiduously overlooks those passages in which Schneider discusses this and other examples and concentrates instead on castigating the equally deliberate affective rhetoric of self-defence.[19] Indeed, he pointedly insists on operating with notions of quality which validate Josef Mengele's totalitarian substantives at the expense of the weary interjection attributed to the son. And in the process he makes his failure to understand what Schneider is doing in *Vati* appear almost wilful.

For *Vati*, far from being an instance of mere opportunistic transposition, entails an act of imaginative re-creation. And what is re-created is precisely the failure out of which *Bunte* has manufactured successful journalism. To that extent it can be described as a 'prä-essayistische', or at least a 'prä-journalistische Erzählung'. It exemplifies the view that it must be hard for a son to measure up to the sensationalized accounts of atrocities attributed to his mythical monstrous father. In that sense *Vati* is not about Josef Mengele, and certainly does not subscribe to the lazy stylization of him as an 'extraordinary real-life person' (Burgess, 119). Rather, it is about the son and the son's capitulations. Hence the allergic reactions of those who believe that the imagination should never be seen to capitulate can be read as paradoxical praise. In other words: if *Vati* is a failure, it is an exemplary failure.

In his defence of *Vati*, Schneider is also concerned to rebut the second of the three charges persistently levelled against him: that of mere opportunistic topicality.[20] Implicit in this is the reproach that even in his so-called 'Erzählungen' Schneider is in fact writing mere ephemeral journalism rather than properly permanent literature. A glance at the subject-matter and settings of

Schneider's earlier 'Erzählungen' particularly would suggest that this is a plausible point of view. The upheavals of the late 1960s which form the background to *Lenz* have soberly celebrated their silver jubilee. The debate about the *Radikalenerlaß* likewise died down long ago and might be seen to have made of the unfortunate Kleff an unemployable anachronism. And what are we to make of the *Mauerspringer* in a world where there is no wall?

On close inspection, however, the impression that Schneider's works owe their success more to their topicality than to any inherent qualities turns out to be wrong. For clearly, even *Lenz* is not about commitment, but about detachment. As in the Büchner, this detachment has something to do with madness, objectivity, and loss. In that sense the atmosphere of Schneider's story is not that of the student revolt itself, but of its aftermath. And such premonitions of an aftermath, it seems to me, are hard to reconcile with the charge of mere topicality. For coming to terms with the ending of something is a timeless and endless experience (especially if, as in the case of Büchner's *Lenz*, that something is the unity of the world guaranteed by God). In other words: it is because Schneider's *Lenz* is ultimately about failure, specifically about the subjective experience of failure, that it can bridge the gap between the author of *Der Hofmeister* and students not yet born in 1968.

The same premonition of an aftermath, this same sense of an ultimate failure underlying all possible or apparent successes is also present in . . . *schon bist du ein Verfassungsfeind*. The carefully judged time sequence of the book culminates in the moment where the judge retires to make a decision which may have the effect of negating the whole process. Just before that happens, the book expresses the possibility of its own uselessness: 'Warum haben Sie eigentlich diesen Haufen Papier nicht als Beweismittel vorgelegt? Beweist er denn gar nichts?' (*VF*, 106). This question in turn is provoked by a strategy whereby the authorities turn an apparent victory into a defeat by simply shifting the goal-posts. And the outburst which that gives rise to goes beyond the immediate occasion to universalize powerlessness and a sense of defeat: 'Ahnungslos waren wir alle, ahnungslos und dumm!' (*VF*, 105.)

In the opening essay of *Extreme Mittellage*, Schneider attributes to history the same mischievousness as had earlier been apparent in the authorities' treatment of Kleff (*EMR*, 7). The refusal by politicians of all parties to admit that they too had been clueless and stupid is seen by Schneider as a symptomatic and serious fault.[21] He himself therefore does not claim prescience. In a paradoxical way, however, he might have done. After all, had not the very attention he lavished on the wall been taken by Werner Herzog as the precondition for the disappearance of that structure?[22] Had he not filled *Der Mauerspringer* with the stories of those who, in their quixotic determination to defy or dismantle the wall, proved that it was at least physically surmountable? And had he not thus looked forward to a time when such people would be left aimless in limbo with only a shadow to contend with? Certainly, the names by which Schneider baptized this shadow and its effects, the 'Krankheit des Vergleichens' and the 'Mauer im Kopf' have proved to be at least as intractably valid in the period since 1989 as they were in the days when the wall still stood (*DMS*, 60 and 102). In that sense, there is something prophetic about the avoidance of the subjunctive in the statement: 'Die Mauer im Kopf einzureißen wird länger dauern, als irgendein Abrißunternehmen für die sichtbare Mauer braucht' (*DMS*, 102). Again it is a premonition of an aftermath, of a success which will point up failures. So it is not for nothing that the final paragraph of *Der Mauerspringer* expresses unsentimental intimations of mortality in a kind of backward-looking future tense, 'als sei ein immer nur gefürchteter Abschied jetzt wahr' (*DMS*, 117–18).

In moving in this way from thoughts about the longevity of the wall to that of his own life, Schneider is laying himself open to another of the charges regularly levelled against him: namely that he frequently moves without prior permission from one side to the other of the wall erected by critics between the private and the political. Thus Buselmeier, despite his apparent acknowledgment of the interdependence of the two spheres, seems to have expected from *Lenz* a full account of what he calls 'die bekannten politischen Daten der Jahre der Revolte'. (Buselmeier, 2). Conversely, behind the grotesque word 'anbalzen' which Schönfeld applies obliquely to *Vati* lies an unspoken irritation that Schneider is there intervening in a sensitive political area in which he has no direct personal experience and therefore no right to speak (Schönfeld, 219). And when Salman Rushdie complains that in the *Wall-Jumper* Schneider 'scarcely ever lets the fiction rip', he is presumably objecting to the way in which we are never allowed to forget that the wall jumped in that work is always at least partly an actual buffer between two political systems.[23]

As we have seen Schneider taking pains to point out, this distinction is a wholly artificial one, based on a fundamental misunderstanding of the relationship between politics and literature. But once it has been set up, it has the effect of marooning the critics themselves on opposite sides of the divide. In the language of *Atempause*, 'Widersprüchlichkeit', or at best 'Unentschiedenheit' is masquerading as 'falsche Zwangsläufigkeit'. And indeed, in one of the central essays of that collection, Schneider duly notes the case of the critic who on different occasions objected with equal virulence to a move in either direction:

> Vor kurzem fragte mich ein Journalist, ob die auch bei mir zu beobachtende Neigung, wieder 'ich' zu sagen, nicht eine Flucht aus der Politik ins Private darstelle. Derselbe Mann hatte acht Jahre zuvor gefragt, ob die Neigung, in der ersten Person Plural zu sprechen, nicht eine Flucht aus privaten Problemen in die Politik darstelle. (*AP*, 162)

The problem, of course, is in the word 'Flucht' and its associated prepositions. And it is a problem which even threatens to undermine the careful argument Colin Riordan constructs on the subject. Thus on the one hand he insists that 'although *Lenz* had been set in 1969, against the scene of much political activity, the hero's inner conflicts in coming to terms with his life are the issues at hand, even though the causes of his personal problems are in the main social and political. Since these problems lie within the individual, and below the surface, that is where they must be examined.' (Riordan, 7). Later in the same paragraph he notes: 'Furthermore, all the stories are about power, and in particular, power struggles between individuals. The importance of power conflicts lies in the fact that they constitute the essence of all political activity' (ibid.). If both these statements are true, which they clearly are, then Riordan's statement in the same passage, that '*Die Wette* represents a retreat into the private sphere' (ibid.) can only mean that in that text Schneider is looking at the continuum of the private and the political as it were from the other end.[24]

And that is precisely the point. For this collection of short stories, published in 1978, seems to me, as to Manfred Bosch, to constitute the fictional equivalent of the collection of essays published the previous year. There are a number of subtle and important parallels between them. Thus where the author of *Atempause* is concerned to distance himself from the way literature is treated

in universities, so in the first story of *Die Wette* Morlock has for-
gotten to remove the title of 'Professor' from the name-plate by
his bell (*DW*, 7). Where *Atempause* contains an essay on film and a
personal anecdote which undermines it, so in the earlier stories of
Die Wette repeated reference is made to the stagy nature of the
events described.[25] Where in *Atempause* the reference to the stut-
terer was seen to touch on the danger of the mimetic fallacy, so
the title of *Die Wette* is resonant with precisely that element of
risk. Where *Atempause* turned on the question of the relationship
between politics and literature, between the private and the public, so the stories of *Die Wette* are shot through with politics in
such a way that the distinction between private and public ceases
to hold good. And where the epigraph of *Atempause* had the effect
of making Schneider's work into a literature of constructive failure, so in *Die Wette* every single story is the story of failure.

Moreover, just as it has been suggested here that *Atempause* is
central to Schneider's work in that it engages with the antinomies
on which the critics based their judgements and hence clarifies
what Schneider is trying to do, so *Die Wette* brings together so
many themes and motifs which occur elsewhere in Schneider's
work that it is hard not to attribute to it some form of central
significance. Thus the Italian stories, 'Zeit zum Sterben' and especially 'Experiment mit mehreren Männern', are reminiscent of the
Italian section of *Lenz*, especially the episode with Pierra. The
Berlin story, 'Verloren im dritten Satz', in which balls move
almost hypnotically backwards and forwards over a resonantly
symbolic barrier, can be seen as a precursor to *Der Mauerspringer*.
Similarly the dogs of 'Zeit zum Sterben' are related generically
and technically to those other dogs of both *Der Mauerspringer* and
Extreme Mittellage.[26] And indeed the episode in *Der Mauerspringer*
in which a border guard barks at a dog also contains a reference
to diving which recalls the title story of *Die Wette*, while the item
which the guards' good humour enables the 'ich' to take across
the wall is a volume of 'Erzählungen' (*DMS*, 90–2).

It was above all the publication of *Paarungen* in 1992, however,
which underlined the importance of *Die Wette*. Thus the related-
ness of (Professor) Morlock from 'Das Ende jeder Diskussion' with
the lecturing Eduard from *Paarungen* is borne out by the fact that
both, confronted on the stairs by possible ghosts of their student-
rebellious past, resort to the same let-out phrase.[27] The story of
Eduard and his three women in *Paarungen* is comparable with that

of Martin and his in 'Experiment mit mehreren Männern' not only
in that the constellation is the same, but also in the narrative perspective used to convey it. The return with a former love to the
country of one's childhood is a pattern which links 'Das Wiedersehen' to Chapter 25 of *Paarungen* – though Klara's maniacal driv-
ing is more akin to that of Vittoria in 'Experiment mit mehreren
Männern'.[28] The statistical reflection on the likely average length
of a love affair which comes near the beginning of *Paarungen*
comes near the end of *Die Wette*.[29] Near the heart of both books is
a bet which also has to do with love. And the rivalry between
Eduard and Lothar in *Paarungen* is prefigured in the longest story
of *Die Wette*: 'Der große und der kleine Bruder'.

This last story has especially exercised the ingenuity of the
critics.[30] They have not been slow to point out that Peter Schneider
too has a brother, Michael, who works in the same field, can be
said to have started later and to have waited longer for his first
success, and who has not been afraid to call into question the
achievements of his sibling. (He is also apparently a practising
magician.)[31] Now the implications of this seemingly clear autobiographical reference would seem to me to be threefold. In the first
place, it would suggest that the other constellations which *Die
Wette* shares with *Paarungen* might be similarly rooted in
Schneider's subjective experience. And that is important not because it underlines the 'autobiographical' aspect of Schneider's
writing in general, but because it corroborates the impression of
the centrality of *Die Wette*. Secondly, if 'Der große und der kleine
Bruder' is read as being about the Schneider brothers, it means
that it must refer at some level to the art they both practise. In
which case, the elder Tarquini's insistence on honesty, skill and an
absence of trickery can be seen to sum up precisely the message of
the first and last essays of *Atempause*. And thirdly, if the 'ich'
which ends the story is identifiable with Peter Schneider, this
provides further proof of the ability of both to contemplate a success which is also a failure. For the elder Tarquini is ultimately
convinced that he has proved himself to be 'der wahre Zauberer';
but only at the expense of an injury which will probably prevent
his ever performing again (*DW*, 97).

In the collection generally, this paradigmatic failure is rehearsed
in the areas not only of art, but also of love, politics and sport.
Thus the title story of the collection is about the 'one that got
away', about a man who paradoxically helps his partner to win a

bet with a possible rival by confirming her view of him as a failure. It is a story which suggests, but never clinches, a parallel
between sporting and sexual prowess. To that extent it invites
comparison with Hemingway, and W. Martin Lüdke, for one, is
not the man to decline such an invitation. But instead of examining the similarities and differences, he merely contents himself
with the canonicizing: 'Mit Hemingway aber sollte Schneider
besser nicht konkurrieren' (Lüdke, 294). Personally, I am far from
convinced that that is what Schneider is doing. Rather, because
the failure of the 'ich' is directly linked to his political insight into
the ecosystem he is invading and to the human face he briefly
attributes to his prey, it can be seen not as ironically, but as paradoxically positive. It is therefore not competing with Hemingway,
but overturning him.[32] And in the process it actually provides
what Lüdke had looked for in vain: an admittedly oblique reference to environmental politics.

In 'Das Ende jeder Diskussion' the reference to politics, as to
sport, as to love, is not so much oblique as sarcastic. Because Morlock offers to co-operate with the two intruders beyond the call of
necessity, he is qualified by them as 'schwul' (*DW*, 14). Earlier, the
rush of verbalization provoked by a nosebleed culminates in a
pair of sentences which cancel each other out in a manner reminiscent of Kafka: 'Er hatte keinerlei Erfahrung in der Erwiderung
physischer Gewalt, aber von nun an würde er sich mit seinen
Mitteln wehren. Es sind nichts als Ausreden, daß ein Geistesarbeiter gegen zwei erfahrene Schläger keinerlei Chancen hat' (*DW*, 11).
In much the same way, the protestations of the allegedly under-
privileged 'Pickelige' are provoked simply by the unfortunate
mislaying of a pistol. Morlock is aware of this, but is none the less
misled by his own *sententiae* into giving the pistol back. Later,
these protestations are revoked by the returning 'Pickelige' and
the discussion Morlock wanted to provoke by his gesture is
reduced to the rhythmic thumping of his head against the door.

Here, it seems to me, an instructive parallel might be drawn
with Frisch's *Biedermann und die Brandstifter*. There too the suggestion that the arsonists might be driven by political motives is
toyed with, presented as an imputation of the prison authorities
and ultimately dismissed in favour of the pleasure principle.[33]
Schneider's description of the giant Harry is also very close to
Frisch's presentation of the equally gigantic Schmitz.[34] The relationship between the giant and the intellectual is also similar. So

too is the fact that it does briefly, but deceptively, appear to be possible for both Morlock and Biedermann to extricate themselves from the situation they find themselves in. Where in the Schneider the distinction between 'Geistesarbeiter' and 'Schläger' proves untenable when the 'Pickelige' turns out to share Morlock's taste in music, so Biedermann's attempts to bring himself down to the level of his 'guests' founder amid the suggestion that at least one of them may be his social equal. But even more significant, it seems to me, is the fact that Morlock, like Biedermann, gets trapped by his phraseology into making himself an accomplice in the destruction of his own flat. For the left-wing intellectual no less than for the phrase-spinning capitalist, failure is pre-programmed in the categories of language used. That it is a political failure, of course, is evident from *Vati*. And the tendency of critics to avoid facing that failure in themselves by ascribing it to the respective author is understandable, but regrettable.[35]

If 'Die Wette' engaged with Hemingway and 'Das Ende jeder Diskussion' with Frisch, 'Verloren im dritten Satz' seems to me to be quintessential Schneider. It is set in Schneider's city of Berlin, in a pocket of resistance to the Ku'damm. The protagonist Charly is likewise fighting a losing battle against change, age, death. His attempt to compact with the first of these is unobtrusively symbolized in his half-hearted determination to replace his old table-tennis bat. The second is already making itself felt in his back and shoulders, and may be impeding his performance by making him tired. It may also contribute to his wife's desire to 'amuse herself a little'. The third has carried off a colleague with a ruptured liver. (Indeed, the interest in the ages at which people died makes a nice comparison with that other obsession, recorded in *Atempause*, with the ages at which they published their first books.) In other words, the unprecedented defeat which Charly suffers at the end of the story is the beginning of an end, the premonition of an aftermath, but also the logical consequence of earlier victories. That it also has a sexual corollary is touched on very briefly. The political dimension too is present not only in the nature of the sport but in Charly's reaction to the left-wing slogans on the radio and in the yellowing of the magazines which Franz reads. More-over, the simple gesture of moving a name with which the story ends is both resonant and reversible: it need mean nothing but can imply a great deal. Like the ending of . . . *schon bist du ein Verfassungsfeind* it keeps open the possibility that the next week's match will overturn the result of this one and the reflections it gave rise to.

In all these respects, Charly's failures are exemplary. The very gesture with which he transmogrifies the aspirations of the workers into military marches exemplifies the double failure of German history. The arena of his initial victories during and just after the war, and hence of his inevitable failure, is a divided island. The failure to convert these early successes into material prosperity, which entails a refusal to build high walls and the creation of a run-down oasis to which former colleagues return, is a quixotic one with a particular resonance in the schizophrenic city. The monomaniacal pursuit of a single talent and the obstinate refusal to give in to weariness and pain will necessarily end in a failure which must be both acknowledged and delayed. The failure to construct a lasting monogamous relationship must be faced and strategies devised for dealing with it. And behind it all, of course, is the knowledge of the ultimate failure, the rupture.

Die Wette was Peter Schneider's third book of fiction. In it he triumphantly draws the portrait of a man who loses in the third set. Implicit in the coincidence, it seems to me, is the essence of Schneider's own gamble: to face up to, to admit to, to write about, and indeed imaginatively to write, failure. As the injuries of the elder Tarquini eloquently remind us, it is a project which requires rare courage. And that, ultimately, is why I am convinced that the author of it is indeed 'der wahre Zauberer'.

Notes

[1] See 'Die Mängel der gegenwärtigen Literaturkritik', *AP*, 9–30.

[2] See 'Die Beseitigung der ersten Klarheit', *AP*, 207–34.

[3] Compare for example: 'Dem Leser bleibt angesichts so vieler Zurücknahmen nichts Besseres übrig, als seinerseits die Lektüre von Mayers Kritik rückgängig zu machen' (*AP*, 22).

[4] Compare for example: 'Einmal in Schwung gekommen, schrieb ich in diese Reden alles hinein, was mich persönlich betraf und empörte' (*AP*, 220).

[5] Compare 'Vom Nutzen des Klischees. Betrachtungen zum Wildwestfilm', *AP*, 42–60, with *AP*, 218.

[6] 'Die Phantasie im Spätkapitalismus und die Kulturrevolution', *AP*, 127–61.

[7] 'Literatur als Widerstand. Am Beispiel von Bert Brechts *Arturo Ui*', *AP*, 111–26, and 'Über den Unterschied von Literatur und Politik', *AP*, 162–74.

[8] Gordon Burgess, 'Was da ist, das ist [nicht] mein', in Arthur Williams *et al.* (eds.), *Literature on the Threshold: The German Novel in the 1980s* (Leamington Spa, Berg, 1990) 107–22 (p. 107).

[9] I am indebted to Dr Mererid Hopwood, Co-ordinator of the Centre for Contemporary German Studies at the University of Wales, Swansea, not least for having supplied me with so much of this material.

[10] Michael Buselmeier, 'Peter Schneider', *Kritisches Lexikon zur deutschsprachigen Gegenwartsliteratur*, ed. Heinz Ludwig Arnold.

[11] Cf. 'Antwort an einen anonymen Kritiker', *AP*, 202–3: 'Die Sache ist aber die, daß der *Lenz* überhaupt keine Autobiographie ist und auch nicht sein wollte' (203).

[12] See Gerda-Marie Schönfeld, 'So eine Nachbarschaft', *Der Spiegel*, 9 March 1987, 216–19; Peter Schneider, 'Vom richtigen Umgang mit dem Bösen', *DÄ*, 82–121 (pp. 98–106,) and Colin Riordan's succinct conflation of these and other sources in Colin Riordan (ed.), *Peter Schneider: Vati* (Manchester, Manchester University Press 1993), 24–5.

[13] Compare the parenthesis in Burgess, 108: '("Plagiarized" would be a more accurate, if more emotive term).'

[14] Compare *BP*, 59–95 and *L*, 13f., 20f., etc.

[15] See 'Bericht über eine Berliner Volksschule', *BP*, 96–125.

[16] Peter Schneider, 'Aufgegebenes Gelände', *Freibeuter* 8 (1981), 55–62, (pp. 55f.).

[17] Peter Schneider, 'Das Licht am Ende des Erzählens', in Heinz Ludwig Arnold (ed.), *Bestandsaufnahme Gegenwartsliteratur* (Munich, edition text + kritik, 1988), 54–60 (p. 60).

[18] Burgess, 117, *V*, 53.

[19] *DÄ*, 116–17; Burgess, 120–2.

[20] The charge is implicit in Schönfeld's viciously disingenuous last paragraph, quoted also in Riordan, 97, and rebutted in *DÄ*, 101.

[21] Compare in particular 'Mann kann sogar ein Erdbeben verpassen', *EMR*, 52–74.

[22] Werner Herzog, 'Absurde Anfälle der Ordnung', *Der Spiegel*, 24 May 1982, 210–13 (p. 210).

[23] Salman Rushdie, 'Tales of Two Berlins', *The New York Times Book Review*, 29 January 1984.

[24] Riordan is by no means the only critic to speak of *Die Wette* in these terms. Compare, for example, Buselmeier, 6: 'Die . . . Machtkämpfe haben sich aus dem politisch-öffentlichen Raum in den privaten verlagert.' Likewise, W. Martin Lüdke freely admits to being disappointed in the volume because 'da ist nicht mehr von Berufsverbot die Rede, keine Spur von irgendwelchen Umweltskandalen, ganz am Rande, fast schon versteckt, in der letzten Erzählung einmal ein schüchterner Hinweis auf die gegenwärtige politische Situation in diesem Lande' (W. Martin Lüdke, 'Mal so, mal so', *DNR* 90 (1979), 291–5 (p. 292)). On the positive side, Manfred Bosch sees in *Die Wette* 'etwas von dieser reflexiven Bedächtigkeit' which shows 'wie fremd Schneider jeder Aktionismus ist' (Manfred

Bosch, 'Von kleinen und großen Fischen', *Die Horen* 114 (1979), 165–6 (p. 165).

[25] Compare for example 'Das Ende jeder Diskussion', *DW*, 7–22, p. 11 ('Gleichzeitig hatte er das deutliche Gefühl, Objekt einer Inszenierung zu sein' and 'was soll das Theater') and p. 18 ('"Ich habe es satt, daß ihr euch hier wie zwei Filmgangster aufführt"').

[26] Compare *DW*, 23ff., *DMS*, 91–2 and *EMR*, 189–94.

[27] Compare *DW*, 10, 'Aber ich muß euch gleich sagen, daß ihr bei mir an der falschen Adresse seid' with *P*, 214: 'Sie meinen nicht mich. Ich bin nicht der Adressat Ihrer Geschichte, sagte er leise.'

[28] Compare *P*, 310 and *DW*, 53–4.

[29] Compare *P*, 14 and *DW*, 99.

[30] Lüdke (295) and Buselmeier (6) single it out for special praise; Bosch (166) regards it as the weak point of the collection.

[31] On this, see particularly the anonymous article 'Unter Brüdern' in *Der Spiegel* , 15 December 1980, 177.

[32] Ten years later, in the *text + kritik* article, p. 58, Schneider rather disparagingly quotes Hemingway on heroism and so lends tenuous support to this view.

[33] Max Frisch, *Biedermann und die Brandstifter*, ed. Peter Hutchinson (London, Methuen, 1986), 84 and 96.

[34] Compare *DW*, 10 with Frisch, 32ff.

[35] Thus it is noticeable that Lüdke's response to 'Das Ende jeder Diskussion' neatly prefigures the louder outcry provoked by *Vati*. His objection that the action for example is 'ohne jede Spannung' overlooks the signpost 'wie lächerlich vorhersehbar alles ist' as assiduously as Burgess overlooks the 'mehr ist mir . . . nicht eingefallen' (Lüdke, 292, *DW*, 12, Burgess, 118, *V*, 53). Similarly Lüdke's complaint that 'die Moral von der Geschichte ist so aufdringlich wie platt' is remarkably close to the reactions recorded in *Deutsche Ängste* to the statement in *Vati* that 'wir sind . . . die Söhne und Töchter der Täter, wir sind nicht die Kinder der Opfer' (Lüdke, 292, *DÄ*, 120, *V*, 42). As Hutchinson shows (6f.), Frisch's play has been rather differently interpreted on either side of the ex-wall.

7

'Die Lustmaschine': Science, Myth and Progress in Peter Schneider's *Paarungen*

COLIN RIORDAN

As its title implies, Peter Schneider's *Paarungen* contains a good deal of sex. One such scene is notable for its combination of mechanistic functionality with mythic overtones: 'Mit raschen, sachkundigen Griffen tat sie, was nötig ist, um einen Mann spitz zu machen, das Programm anzuwerfen. Suchte und fand die Stellung, die ein Minimum an eigener Bewegung erforderte. Aus Intuition, aus jahrtausendealter Erfahrung schien sie die Knöpfe zu kennen, die die Lustmaschine bewegen' (*P*, 198). This cybernetic notion of the man as a machine to be programmed, and of male sexual desire as a technological artefact, contrasts with the well-worn image of the intuitive woman as a mythical archetype stretching through millenniums of human experience. The implied conjoinment of science and myth in an analysis of human sexual relations characterizes the whole novel, and conditions one of the fundamental questions which the novel addresses: the nature of progress itself. In this chapter I should like to argue that science and myth are paradoxically linked throughout *Paarungen*, that this link emerges in large part through literary allusion, and that the effect is to supply an answer to the question of whether changes in human affairs (either personal or geo-political) must incrementally be for the better.

Given that Schneider has himself undergone considerable political transformations over the years, it would perhaps not be surprising if he were to regard the possibility of human progress towards a more perfect future with favour. For progress implies the ability to learn from past mistakes and to avoid them thereafter. In an essay which first appeared in 1993, Schneider argued that error can be a positive characteristic: 'Intelligente und erkannte Irrtümer gehören eigentlich zum Besten, was Menschen

hervorzubringen vermögen; die Irrtümer kommen in ihrer Wich-
tigkeit gleich nach den Erkenntnissen, weil sie deren Bedingung
sind' (*VEG*, 20).[1] Schneider's view is clear enough; whether the
central character of his novel bears out the argument is another
matter, for there is no necessity for an author to share the opin-
ions or approve of the actions of his characters. Furthermore,
although the novel (his first work designated as such) appeared in
1992, only a year before the essay quoted above, it was actually
begun and is set ten years earlier. Indeed, the story may well have
been gestating for almost twenty years.

It was in 1974 that Schneider published his essay 'Die Sache mit
der "Männlichkeit". Gibt es eine Emanzipation der Männer?'.[2]
Drawing on Wilhelm Reich's *Die sexuelle Revolution*,[3] this early
essay considers the way in which sexual relationships between
men and women are still regulated by unchanging human needs
even though traditional norms and roles had by the early 1970s
been subjected to widespread criticism or been rejected. Much of
the analysis of feminism and of changing masculine identity has
been thoroughly superseded by subsequent developments in gen-
der theory. However, the difficulties which, in Schneider's view at
that time, men experienced in achieving 'Harmonie zwischen
ihrem Geschlechts- und ihrem Gefühlsleben' (*BP*, 242) seem dur-
able enough to have permeated the plot of *Paarungen*. Moreover, a
question posed early in the 1974 essay – 'sich trennen oder
zusammenbleiben?' (*BP*, 212) – was to become the ostensible *raison
d'être* of the 1993 novel. The discussions which arise from this
question are described in the essay as 'Die zahllosen Streit- und
Versöhnungsgespräche, die sich jetzt in Kneipen und Wohn-
gemeinschaften abspielen' (*BP*, 213), and form the common thread
linking a host of varied themes in the later novel.

Readers of *Paarungen* will know that one of many pub conver-
sations between three friends, Eduard (through whose eyes the
story is largely told), Theo and André turns to the question of
why relationships between men and women break down so
regularly. They whimsically conclude that their whole generation
is the subject of an experiment in male-female relations. In an
attempt to supply proof for this contention, each of them wagers
that he will remain with his partner for a year, on pain of paying
for a ski-ing holiday for six. Each has his own strategy, but most
readers will guess that all are doomed to fail. At the end of the
novel none has won the bet, while all have been stripped of their

pride and their cash by a resourceful but unscrupulous young
woman they meet by chance in Warsaw. The bones of the story,
then, rely on one of the oldest conundrums in human history, the
travails of love, and it is here that most of the material for the
comic elements of the novel reside. The serious themes emerge in
the polemics on the ethics of science (Eduard is a molecular biologist), but are both transformed and complemented by the literary
allusions.

Such allusions are, of course, by no means a novelty in
Schneider's work. The cult success of Schneider's first work of fiction, *Lenz*, was quickly complemented by academic interest in the
relation to its literary forebear Büchner's *Lenz*. In *Paarungen*,
Schneider once more overtly engages with the German literary
tradition. Undeterred by the controversy over *Vati* in 1987, when
he was accused of plagiarism for having not named his sources in
a work of fiction,[4] Schneider draws on a number of literary pre-
cedents, most obviously E. T. A. Hoffmann. Perhaps it was the
very obviousness of the reference – in the first few pages Eduard
Hoffmann observes a young woman reading *Die Serapionsbrüder* –
which led a number of reviewers to disparage the allusions con-
temptuously. Given the wholly unfavourable nature of her review
of *Paarungen*, it is hardly surprising that Iris Radisch should sneer
at Schneider's alleged 'leere, aber bedeutsame Anspielungen auf
die Romanwelt und die Figuren E. T. A. Hoffmanns'.[5] Other
reviewers were less scornful, but Werner Fuld in the *Frankfurter
Allgemeine* was also unconvinced by Schneider's allusions to
Hoffmann: 'Er läßt in Eduards Kneipe eine junge Frau
E. T. A. Hoffmanns *Serapionsbrüder* lesen und verteilt die Initialen
seiner männlichen Akteure (Eduard, Theo, André) so, daß sie den
Anfangsbuchstaben des romantischen Dichternamens entsprechen;
zu allem Überfluß heißt Eduard noch Hoffmann mit Nachnamen,
aber dieses literar-historische Vexierspiel führt im Roman zu
nichts. Es ist ein totes Motiv.'[6] Fuld could also have pointed out
that both Klara and Lothar (Eduard's girlfriend and brother) are
names from *Der Sandmann*, while Theodor and Lothar are both
names of characters in *Die Serapionsbrüder*. Indeed, the critic may
have a point with his accusation that Schneider is over-egging the
Hoffmann pudding, for there is more of the Romantic writer even
than this.

In *Paarungen*, Schneider imitates the style and structure of Hoffmann's writing, thereby consciously acknowledging an influence

which was present in previous works (especially *Der Mauer-springer*) but of which, according to his own account, he had been unaware.[7] The mysterious stranger who appears from nowhere to sow disaster and destroy happiness, familiar from the works of E. T. A. Hoffmann, is present in *Paarungen* as a 'Spaltpilz', a 'Trennungsvampir', who appears without warning, causes couples to split by telling a subversive story, and disappears after ruining their bliss (see *P*, 49). The narrative structure of *Die Serapionsbrüder* is imitated, in that friends meet in cosy sodality to tell each other extraordinary stories. And few readers could miss the modern version of *Der Sandmann*, Theo's story of how he was tricked by his wife and subsequently entrapped by the *Stasi*, who use a beautiful, but strangely lifeless, agent called Olympia to unsettle Theo and tempt him into betrayal of the state. E. T. A. Hoffmann's influence is detectable even in the style, especially in the repeated use of 'seltsam' and 'merkwürdig'.

It would be tempting to dismiss such allusions as mere whimsy, particularly since they are so obvious to any reader with even a slight knowledge of the German literary tradition that little pleasure is to be gained from successfully detecting their presence. However, to reject the Hoffmann dimension on those grounds or because Schneider is allegedly wearing his learning heavily would not do the novel justice. There is a sense in which the 'Sonderstatus' of Berlin before the reunification of Germany did give rise to extraordinary stories and extraordinary events, giving sustenance to a literary representation of the city which draws on the E. T. A. Hoffmann tradition. A story populated by exotic and mysterious figures who disappear as suddenly as they have come on the scene, and who tell fantastic tales the veracity of which cannot be satisfactorily established: all of this was possible in the Berlin of pre-1989. Anyone with the ability to go freely from West Berlin to the GDR could appear and disappear mysteriously, as Theo does. And the *Stasi* were certainly capable of engineering an apparently fantastic series of events for purposes unknowable to the victims. The world of E. T. A. Hoffmann, then, is entirely appropriate given the setting of *Paarungen*.

However, the aptness of the Hoffmann model on its own is not a strong enough argument to refute the criticism that these allusions constitute 'ein totes Motiv'. For it is only in combination and in contrast with other literary allusions in the novel that the Hoffmann dimension becomes a powerful literary dynamic in a

way which goes beyond merely reflecting unexpected parallels
between the skewed logic of life in 1980s West Berlin and the
bizarre fantasies of the Romantic writer. The other obvious literary
antecedent from the German literary tradition, noticed by a far
smaller number of reviewers, is Goethe's *Die Wahlverwandtschaften.*[8] Here too there is a coincidence of names, in particular
that of the main character Eduard. Even Eduard's experimental
white mouse in *Paarungen*, which tantalizingly offered proof of an
antigen to multiple sclerosis before escaping in a raid by animal
liberationists, is called Lotte, comically echoing the Charlotte who
is Eduard's wife in the classic novel. But there are other more
important parallels. The most obvious is thematic. It was Goethe's
novel that set the standard in the German tradition for treatment
of the permanence, impermanence and changing nature of
male–female relationships, and in particular the problem of marriage and children.

Perhaps the most famous words from *Die Wahlverwandtschaften*
are the most misused: 'Die Ehe ist der Anfang und der Gipfel aller
Kultur.'[9] Naturally, the upshot of the novel is in fact that marital
bonds may not be able to withstand the strength of human
passion. In Goethe's novel the sanctity of marriage is only gradu-
ally undermined, whereas in *Paarungen* it is dismissed from the
start. But the notion that apparently stable relationships may
either be destroyed or strengthened by unexpected outside influence is present in both. Furthermore, despite the Hoffmannesque
overtones, Schneider's 'Spaltpilz' clearly derives its inspiration
from the Count and Baroness in *Die Wahlverwandtschaften*. Mittler,
who (as his name implies) performs exactly the opposite function
to Schneider's 'Spaltpilz', healing divisions and preventing
divorces, denounces the imminent arrival of the Count and Baroness on Eduard's estate: 'nehmt euch in acht: sie bringen nichts als
Unheil! Ihr Wesen ist wie ein Sauerteig, der seine Ansteckung
fortpflanzt!'[10] Just as the 'Spaltpilz' (or 'wandelnder Virus', as he is
also described; see *P*, 49) multiplies his effects through infection,
so too do the Count and Baroness in Mittler's eyes. But the whimsical 'Spaltpilz' and the rather more serious fears of Mittler point
to an important dimension of *Die Wahlverwandtschaften* which is
echoed as a serious theme in Schneider's novel: the ethics of scientific progress.

In Goethe's day, nothing was known of viruses, but the action
of yeast in replicating itself in the right circumstances had been

familiar for centuries. This parallel is merely part of a much broader picture in which the effects of new insights into chemical and biological processes on society and human relationships are investigated in both novels. It is in this area that the importance of Schneider's debt to Goethe emerges, and in which new light is cast on the allusions to E. T. A. Hoffmann. Although Goethe was interested in alchemy, and took it seriously as a discipline, there is little or no evidence of this in *Die Wahlverwandtschaften*. The novel was written as Goethe worked on *Zur Farbenlehre*, and the treatment of science in the novel is evidently fundamental to the analysis of human relations. Indeed, it is clear that the problem of cool intellect versus intelligent emotion, *ratio* against 'gefühlvolles Vernünfteln', as Benjamin put it in his seminal essay on *Die Wahlverwandtschaften*, both substantiates and transcends the theme of the novel.[11] The efforts of humankind not only to understand but to impose its will on the natural environment, which characterized the Enlightenment and paved the way for the Industrial Revolution, are evident in the desire of Charlotte and Eduard to landscape their estate. The Hauptmann, as the primary architect of the work, is able to survey and alter the topography of the estate by means of his knowledge of recent technology. And it is the Hauptmann who sets out for the benefit of Eduard and Charlotte the chemical processes which become the explicit analogy for the changing human relationships in the novel. Eduard remarks that sexual relationships might be used as an example to explain the tendency of separate substances in combination to form new compounds: 'wie diese durch Sitten und Gesetze vereinbar sind, so gibt es auch in unserer chemischen Welt Mittelglieder, dasjenige zu verbinden, was sich aneinander abweist.'[12] The Hauptmann agrees: 'Diejenigen Naturen, die sich beim Zusammentreffen einander schnell ergreifen und wechselseitig bestimmen, nennen wir verwandt.'[13]

Significantly, it is Eduard who remarks that the complicated cases are the most important: 'die Verwandtschaften werden erst interessant, wenn sie Scheidungen bewirken.'[14] This sentence could stand as the motto for Schneider's *Paarungen*, and it invests Eduard Hoffmann's whimsical efforts to analyse human sexual pairings statistically at the beginning of Schneider's novel with a new significance, for the relationship between scientific and sociological knowledge is thus pushed into the foreground. The Hauptmann uses the example of a chemical reaction between chalk and sulphuric acid in order to explain the meaning of the word 'Wahlverwandtschaft': 'Hier ist eine Trennung, eine neue Zusammensetzung entstanden, und man glaubt sich nunmehr berechtigt, sogar das Wort Wahlverwandtschaft anzuwenden, weil es wirklich aussieht, als wenn ein Verhältnis dem andern vorgezogen, eins vor dem andern erwählt wurde.'[15] Charlotte, however, objects that people are more complicated, and is especially concerned that it matters more if people separate and recombine than if chemical substances do the same: 'Mir sind leider Fälle genug bekannt, wo eine innige, unauflöslich scheinende Verbindung zweier Wesen durch gelegentliche Zugesellung eines dritten aufgehoben und eins der erst so schön verbundenen ins lose Weite hinausgetrieben ward.'[16] Not only does this show even more clearly the origin of Schneider's 'Spaltpilz', but it confirms that for Goethe, the boundaries between scientific enquiry and the complicated and unpredictable behaviour of human beings are less clear than they would appear today. Aesthetics and science are merely variants of the same epistemological tools in Goethe's day. Yet even in modern times, the distinction is not as clear as we might like to think. Art and literature still represent and interpret the complexity of human society and human relationships. That society and those relationships depend on sexual reproduction and on the social structures which arise in order to embrace the process and result of reproduction. At the beginning of the nineteenth century the details of sexual reproduction were ill-understood; Goethe's analogy with chemical processes was the nearest to a scientific view of human relationships that could reasonably be envisaged.

Admittedly, it is in the nature of things that similar limits to scientific knowledge should still exist; the Institute at which Eduard works builds on the discovery by Joshua Lederberg that single-cell micro-organisms also have sexual characteristics, but: 'Die Gesetze, nach denen sich die Bakterien und Hefen anzogen und abstießen, waren jedoch nur zum Teil erklärt' (P, 72). Nevertheless, in our days, the complex workings of sexual reproduction have been revealed to an extent unimaginable two hundred years previously. In the same way as the Hauptmann is able to predict the outcome of chemical reactions, or assess and remodel the topography of the estate, so modern scientists are able to describe and change the genetic constitution of organisms.

The study of genetics at a molecular level is the modern equivalent of Goethe's analogy. Eduard Hoffmann, of course, is a molecular biologist who discovers and loses a cure for multiple sclerosis, and who argues with his brother about nature versus nurture. But in Schneider's novel, in contrast to *Die Wahlverwandtschaften*, it is the science, rather than human relationships, which is invested with a moral dimension. In the late twentieth century, doubts about the ethics of scientific research compete with the supposed advantages in ways which would have been inconceivable at the beginning of the last century, before the publication of the *Origin of Species*.[17] The particular problem in Germany is that for historical reasons this well-known dilemma has been imbued with an ideological passion which places uncomfortable constraints on reasonable discussion of the problem.

In this respect it is worth noting that Eduard Hoffmann is not the only scientist to be a main protagonist in Schneider's work. The central figure in the screenplay of *Messer im Kopf* (1979) is a biochemist, also called Hoffmann, who, like Eduard, was engaged in a research project about 'das Altern der Zellen'.[18] *Messer im Kopf* clearly drew its inspiration from the brain damage suffered by Rudi Dutschke after being shot by a right-wing protester, and Hoffmann's status as a scientist in *Messer im Kopf* is a more peripheral matter than that of the *Paarungen* character, particularly since he has lost the use of his normal intellectual faculties for most of the screenplay. The problematic link between scientific endeavour and political ideology is, however, clear. In particular, the potential benefits of Hoffmann's research, and the damage caused to that potential by his shooting, are lost in the welter of accusation and counter-accusation as each side tries to appropriate Hoffmann for their own ideological ends. That Schneider chose to give the hero of *Paarungen* the name Hoffmann and make him a molecular biologist is clearly part of an attempt to develop a line of thought which had been a preoccupation for a decade or more.

The other scientist to figure prominently in Schneider's work is the Josef Mengele figure in *Vati*, the Auschwitz doctor who is visited by his son while in hiding in Brazil. The uproar which arose even before the publication of this text was a symptom of the difficulties experienced in post-war Germany in discussing the legacy of Auschwitz.[19] The accusations of plagiarism did not find general support, though most reviewers took the precaution of lambasting the piece on literary grounds. The after-effects of that incident are clearly visible in *Paarungen*, and will be returned to below. But the *Vati* row tended to overshadow the salient fact that the Mengele figure in the text is a geneticist.

Like the historical Mengele, the father in Schneider's text regards himself as no more than an entirely objective scientist who is forced to set emotion aside for the greater good. He sees himself as persecuted, and regards his persecution as evidence of a great personal sacrifice made for the good of humankind. This allows him to place himself in a category with the great figures of scientific history who have paid dearly for their revolutionary discoveries, in particular Giordano Bruno and Charles Darwin (*V*, 64). But this is only part of the father's self-mythologizing. Later in the same scene, the potency of the mixture of myth and intellect which characterizes his approach becomes yet more evident. Paradoxically, the father is superficially arguing for the opposite, namely that humankind should reject all 'Mythologien, die ihn zum höchsten Ziel einer gottgewollten Schöpfung erhoben'.[20] As anyone familiar with Nazi ideology would expect, this alleged rejection of mythology is immediately replaced with a further myth: that of the absolute supremacy of natural selection. In a direct quotation from the letters of the historical Josef Mengele, the father argues as follows:

> Die moderne Naturwissenschaft hat den Menschen dieses Jahrhunderts an einen Scheideweg geführt. Entweder entwickelt er endlich ein Wertesystem, das den erkannten Gesetzen der Erbbiologie entspricht, oder er wird von diesen Gesetzen zermalmt. Diese Tat allerdings setzt voraus, daß wir die Gesetze der Natur über die des Menschen stellen und uns, wie Giordano Bruno, lieber verbrennen lassen, als ihnen abzuschwören. (*V*, 66–7)

Leaving aside the terrible irony of the last few words, it is clear that in the familiar ring of Nazi ideology the myth of 'die Gesetze der Natur' is constructed in order to remove all ethical limits on scientific investigation. It emerges from passages elsewhere in the text that the father's concept of genetics is deeply flawed, relying heavily on the irrational myths of nineteenth-century German nationalism. This is a reflection of the approach to science of the historical Mengele, whose grotesque efforts to prove the primacy of heredity in the acquisition of human characteristics not only caused agonies of suffering, but amounted to scientific mumbo-jumbo.[21] This mixture of myth and *ratio* is a defining characteristic of Nazi ideology. It tends to lead those in its thrall to persist in asserting the correctness of their views, whatever the evidence. This is certainly the case for the father in *Vati*, as it was for the historical Mengele. But such a mixture does not only have to be associated with dictatorship and tyranny. Whenever ideology is present, a tendency to mythologize may arise. Where this mythology meets scientific endeavour, the results can be disastrous.

Without drawing egregious parallels between Nazi Germany and the Federal Republic of 1983, it is clear that the problem of myth and *ratio* is present in both. In particular it is a problem of modern science, of which genetics is the best, and in Germany the most explosive, example. The specific German form of opposition to research in genetics is analysed in *Paarungen* as 'eine unerklärte Form der Vergangenheitsbewältigung' (*P*, 227). According to this view, opponents suspect German scientists of secretly pursuing the eugenic aims of Nazi plans, even though German scientists had, by reason of this very legacy, constructed a sophisticated system of safeguards designed to prevent any abuses. That opposition nevertheless arises is ascribed to a process which Schneider had identified in 1988, in the wake of the *Vati* débâcle, and had termed 'Unschuldswahn'.[22] This adds a unique dimension to the debate on scientific ethics in Germany: 'Doch die Debatte war hierzulande durch den Umstand vergiftet, daß die Ankläger für sich ein moralisches Monopol beanspruchten. Sie glaubten, ihre besondere historische Sensibilität unter Beweis zu stellen, indem sie ziemlich wahllos auf Leute zeigten, die angeblich die Verbrechen der Vergangenheit wiederholten' (*P*, 227). But it is also true that this process involves an element of mythologizing, which allows even those who have an understanding of the scientific problems involved to be distracted from the true state of affairs. Eduard is shocked that it is possible for students of biology to mount a protest against his research, given that the outcome is in all probability likely to remain in the realms of pure science, and that any practical application can only be wholly beneficial. But what Eduard does not appreciate is the significance of the fact that the students who carry out the protest are wearing Mickey Mouse masks.

The four students who occupy the front row of Eduard's last lecture of the semester unroll a banner reading: 'Schluß mit den Mäuse-KZs! Freiheit und Glück für alle Labormäuse!' (*P*, 184). Without forgetting that *Paarungen* is a comic novel, it is worth

observing that the incongruous and apparently insensitive con-
junction of Mickey Mouse and concentration camps by the protesters is more than an implied reference to supposed parallels
between Nazi *Erbforschung* and modern genetics research. In the
more than sixty years since its inception, the figure of Mickey
Mouse has become a representative cultural icon which has
usurped previous mythological figures. The cultural reach of
Disney's anthropomorphism has become so widespread and pro-
found in the late twentieth century that our susceptibility to its
implications has been highly sensitized, though perhaps not at the
conscious level. The idea of animals which appear in a parody of
human form, and which have human characteristics and capabil-
ities, is, of course, a staple element of all human mythology. But
whereas in earlier centuries scientific knowledge was not popu-
larly available, and so myth remained accepted on its own terms,
in the late twentieth century such mythical archetypes encroach
dangerously on the territory of scientific research. For Mickey
Mouse, the talking, thinking animal figure, is merely a lovable
variant, or obverse allotrope, of much more sinister figures. In no
other branch of scientific research, except perhaps for artificial
intelligence, is the potential for introducing powerful, fear-induc-
ing mythical archetypes so great as in genetics. I refer to archetypes represented in the figures, for example, of the bogeyman,
the zombie, the Golem, or, of course, Frankenstein. The notion of
a human form which possesses some of the external features but
lacks the essence of humanity gives rise to atavistic fears which
cool intellect is hard put to allay. And when the suspicion arises
that human intellect may be able to create such a form by mis-
using scientific knowledge, then forces come into being which are
readily harnessed by ideological interests.

There are enough examples of science being misused in the
name of ideology in German history to give German scientists in
particular a powerful interest in unshackling their research from
the dictates of ideology. The effort to distinguish between the
costs and benefits of scientific research without being influenced
by myth-driven ideology emerges in *Paarungen* in the literary
allusions. It is this effort which transforms the allusions to E. T. A.
Hoffmann, and in particular to *Der Sandmann*, from the level of a
'totes Motiv' to an important constituting element of the novel. In
stark contrast to Goethe's clear-headed, scientifically knowledge-
able Enlightenment figures in *Die Wahlverwandtschaften* – in

particular the Hauptmann – E. T. A. Hoffmann's image of the scientist is deliberately disturbing. The chemical experiments carried out by Coppelius bear little relation to the soberly scientific, if animated, approach of the Hauptmann, whose chemical reactions could easily be reproduced by any reader. The sinister, mysterious and mystical nature of Coppelius's activities imparts an alchemical dimension to his science. Yet at the same time it is clear that he is a scientist, and that he does possess powerful scientific insights. It is the deliberate mystification of science which makes Coppelius so unsettling a scientist figure. This contrast is even more marked in the case of Spalanzani, introduced in the story as 'der berühmte Professor Physices, Spalanzani'.[23] Spalanzani creates Olimpia using the technology which is available at the time: clockwork. She is an automaton, who owes her existence to the scientist's technological skills. Olimpia, though in part a comic creation, is probably as powerful a figure as any in the German tradition to arouse fears of the misuse of science. While there are clearly mystical elements to Spalanzani's activities (or at least Nathanael perceives them as such), there is no suggestion that Olimpia is alive, or has been called into being by some supernatural process: she is clearly a product of science, and represents the sinister developments of which science is capable in the wrong hands. The parallels with the fears of modern protesters concerning the research of geneticists are clear enough. Olimpia's destructive power is apparent in a number of ways; Nathanael is seduced into madness, and the scene which tips him over the edge involves Olimpia smashing a bench full of scientific apparatus as Coppola and Spalanzani fight over her. While she is a 'leblose Puppe',[24] her manipulator is both malicious and dangerous. Furthermore, it seems likely that Hoffmann was alluding to the historical scientist, Lazzaro Spallanzani, whose work centred on the problems of the origin of life and the possibility of artificial insemination.

The allusions to *Die Wahlverwandtschaften* on the one hand and to *Der Sandmann* on the other thus meet on common ground in the area of science. 'Meet' is perhaps the wrong word, however, for in fact a tension arises between the two which characterizes the whole of *Paarungen*. While Goethe's novel is characterized by a rational approach to science, in which human knowledge is used to further the lot of the characters, and to impose man's will advantageously on the environment, nothing could be further removed from the approach detectable in E. T. A. Hoffmann's work, and particularly in *Der Sandmann*. Here, science is inextricably linked with the supernatural, with the suggestion not that dark forces lie outside human beings, but that dark forces within our own psyche may be unlocked under certain circumstances. In *Der Sandmann*, it is clear that those circumstances include the pursuit of scientific knowledge. In *Paarungen*, then, by implication, the shadow of the mad scientist bent on dangerous self-aggrandizement is juxtaposed with that of the trustworthy, virtuous, white-coated figure who is working for progress and the good of humanity. The question is, which one of these emerges victorious? The obvious answer would be the forces of good; but in fact, the analysis in the novel is not quite that simple. In order to decide the issue, it is necessary to examine the running disputes between the two brothers in the text of *Paarungen*, as well as the developments in Eduard's own views.

Disagreements between brothers are a repeated feature of Schneider's work, reflecting a biographical element which has been present since the 1970s. Michael Schneider's rather negative analysis of *Lenz*[25] written the year after its appearance may have struck home, for in the collection *Die Wette* (1978), Peter Schneider included a story entitled 'Der große und der kleine Bruder' which was clearly a fictional representation of his own relationship with his brother. In that story the elder brother, a stage magician and juggler whose trick was to catch a flying bullet in his teeth, explains to a court that his younger brother, who has followed in his footsteps as a performer, had shot him in the jaw in a desperate effort to prove that the elder brother's trick was achieved by cheating, rather than genuine talent.[26] Michael Schneider struck back with the novella *Das Spiegelkabinett* in 1980, in which the elder brother is shown to be a hopeless megalomaniac.[27] The feud appeared to be in abeyance during the rest of the 1980s, at least in public, although it could be argued that Peter Schneider's *Vati* (1987) may be read as a reply to Michael's essay 'Väter und Söhne posthum'.[28] The relevance of the history of this dispute to the treatment of science in *Paarungen* may not be immediately obvious, but in fact, a core point of disagreement has to do with genetics, and in particular, the nature versus nurture debate. Michael Schneider focused on this in *Das Spiegelkabinett*, and it is this which once more forms the central point of dispute between the brothers in *Paarungen*. Indeed, parts of *Paarungen* are clearly intended as a direct, if rather belated, reply to Michael Schneider's novella.[29] Consider the point in *Das Spiegelkabinett* where the first-person narrator, the younger brother, realizes for the first time that his brother owed his superior skills not only to cheating, but to favouritism on the part of their father, who had selected him to carry on the family tradition of juggling skills:

> Sein sprichwörtliches Ballgefühl war ihm also keineswegs angeboren; es war ihm buchstäblich *anerzogen* worden durch meinen Vater . . . so mußte ich nun mir selbst und meinen Eltern beweisen, daß der Satz: »Der eine hat's, und der andere hat's nicht!«, der die Menschheit letztlich in zwei Rassen teilt, . . . keine Gültigkeit mehr besaß, daß *Arbeit* und *Vertrauen* die alleinigen Erzeuger all jener außergewöhnlichen Talente sind, für deren Dasein wie für deren Fehlen die Menschen gleichermaßen das »Blut«, das »Erbgut«, den »angeborenen Charakter«, die »Rasse«, das »Schicksal« oder die »Vorsehung« verantwortlich machen. Ich mußte beweisen, daß kein Talent vom Himmel fällt, daß das Talent des Menschen vielmehr der Mensch selbst ist.[30]

The attempt to associate the genetic theory of human characteristics with Nazi ideology is clear enough in this quotation, and finds a response in *Paarungen*, in which the nature of scientific knowledge and the way in which it may be influenced by an undeclared sub-text is exemplified by the quarrel between Eduard and his brother Lothar. In this case, both are experts on research into twins; Eduard as a geneticist, and Lothar as a sociologist. Unsurprisingly, Eduard is a supporter of the Minneapolis twins experiments which appear to show that twins separated at birth by some chance nevertheless develop extraordinarily similar characteristics even though they have no contact and grow up in entirely separate environments. In his refutation of the arguments, however, Lothar contends that proof exists that Bouchard's Minneapolis experiments are funded by the CIA, and that the results are falsified. At no point are the substantive issues debated in a scientific manner. In fact, Eduard suspects that the quest for human knowledge in this case is being subverted by an entirely separate agenda:

> Eduard reagierte auf solche Einwände regelmäßig mit einer Heftigkeit, die sich aus dem Gegenstand allein nicht erklärte. Er glaubte zu wissen, worauf Lothars Polemik gegen die »Genfraktion« im Grunde zielte: Es war das »angeborene Talent«, das der Vater Eduard

zugeschrieben hatte . . . In Eduards Fall sei der Talentbonus eindeutig auf eine Wunschbildung des Vaters zurückzuführen . . . Lothar verstieg sich bei seiner Verteidigung der Milieutheorie zu der Behauptung: Ja, durchaus – wäre er, Lothar, im Hause Mozart oder Einstein aufgewachsen, so hätte er der Welt unfehlbar die gleichen Leistungen beschert, die dem angeblichen Genie dieser Männer zugeschrieben würden. (*P*, 27–8)

The tendentious nature of both of these passages (the second clearly a response to the first) reflects the problems raised by the conjoinment of ideology and science in Germany. The implied association of Nazism with genetic theory in the *Spiegelkabinett* passage and the *reductio ad absurdum* approach in the *Paarungen* passage are both the result of ideological pressures of which the brothers in each case are at best only partially aware. The arguments on each side clearly fall into political categories on the left and the right. Yet this is not the whole story, for Eduard is by no means portrayed as being inclined to right-wing politics. On the contrary, he is a leftish relic of 1968 who has become rather more centrist as the years have gone by. In fact, his views derive from scientific knowledge rather than political conviction. It is Lothar who is portrayed as almost obsessive in his determination to show that genetic influences do not determine human characteristics, actuated, Eduard believes, by jealousy over their father's attitude to the elder brother's ability. What is interesting, then, about the genetics debate is not the reasons why the brothers disagree, but that neither of them has any prospect of convincing the other during this perennial dispute. Neither brother is prepared to give ground or to admit weakness or mistake. A proportion of the problem lies in the long-standing sibling rivalry which is evident in the presentation of both characters. Yet both are scientists (insofar as sociology may be termed a science), and thus might be expected to confine their dispute to a more detached plane. Indeed, they exchange research papers from sources appropriate to their standpoint. The problem is that the scientific arguments are subordinated to an ideology which neither brother is able to transcend. And in each case the ideology is supported by evidence which has mythic qualities.

While the somewhat anecdotal nature of the sociological evidence adduced by Lothar may easily be nurtured into the status of myth (the story of twins raised separately who nevertheless have identical tastes has an irresistible attraction about it), it is less easy to see how this could apply to the scientific research pursued by Eduard. However, it is clear from the text that Eduard's pursuit of a genetic cause for multiple sclerosis is itself a kind of search for a Holy Grail, especially since the hoped-for result is so tantalizingly out of reach. Eduard's research is actually characterized by its lack of practical application; any benefit to mankind which accrues is entirely fortuitous. Indeed, Eduard believes that the serendipitous approach of pure science is more likely to yield a useful result than teleological research programmes (see *P*, 76). The kind of science which Eduard pursues thus takes on a quasi-religious aura: 'Grundlagenforscher waren seiner Ansicht nach seltsame Leute; man konnte meinen, sie gehörten einer weltlichen Mönchskaste an. Sie investierten ihren Fleiß, ihre Erfindungsgabe, ihre Gesundheit und übrigens auch beachtliche Summen an Geld in ein Unternehmen, das außer Erkenntnis und Anerkennung kaum einen Gewinn versprach' (*P*, 76–7). A search for something the existence or even the identity of which is not certain has distinct mythical overtones: the implication in *Paarungen* is that pure science, and hence scientific progress, depend on at least the underlying awareness of the possibility that some unexpected find might be made. In this sense, the philosopher's stone is still with us.

Since myths derive their potency from conviction rather than reasoned argument, both the scientific and the sociological approach to the problem of heredity are beset by mutually exclusive mythical archetypes which force the proponents of each argument to deny the possibility of error on their own side, or of merit on the other. It is thus in the nature of things that the problem cannot be solved and that both brothers must insist on their view of events, as does the Mengele figure in *Vati*. It is this inability to admit error on which, in conclusion, I should like to focus. For in the early 1990s, following the collapse of communism in Eastern Europe, this was a problem which Schneider repeatedly addressed in essay form.

Faced with proof, in his view incontrovertible by all reasonable standards, that many of the insights of the political right had been correct, in contrast to the arguments of the left, with respect to Eastern European socialism, Schneider published an essay in *Die Zeit* in 1990 entitled 'Man kann sogar ein Erdbeben verpassen. Plädoyer für eine Vergangenheitsbewältigung der Linken'.[31] In it

Schneider argues not only that every thinker has the right to change an opinion, but that it is desirable that great events should bring such change about. Schneider uses the scientific method as an example of such good practice, where there is no shame attached to the revision or discarding of a previously held hypothesis:

> In den Naturwissenschaften entfällt ein Hauptteil der Arbeit auf die Irrtumsermittlung: dort gibt es kaum einen Erkenntnisfortschritt, ohne daß falsche oder unbrauchbar gewordene Hypothesen benannt und verworfen werden. Was ich hier aufs Korn nehme, ist gerade nicht die Änderung von Meinungen oder Überzeugungen, sondern der lautlose Vollzug: das Vermauscheln der Widersprüche zwischen früher und jetzt vertretenen Standpunkten, das möglichst unauffällige Hinüberrutschen in den Jetzt-Zustand. (*EM*, 56–7)

Few would contest the legitimacy of the argument, and it would be difficult to accuse Schneider of being prone to the same fault: over the years, he has been conspicuously ready to draw attention to his change of views from the earlier Maoist to his present liberal-centrist position. What is less convincing is the analogy with science. The history of science abounds with figures who have clung obstinately to a hypothesis, usually one for which they were originally responsible, in the face of overwhelming evidence to the contrary. For our purposes, perhaps the most apposite example is that of Goethe himself.

While some of Goethe's own scientific work contained original ideas which proved to be of lasting value, he was no adherent of the scientific method as it came to be commonly accepted. Indeed, he was vehemently opposed to Newton's theory of light, in part precisely because the English scientist did use experimental and hypothetical methodology which would be recognizable to the modern scientist but which clashed violently with Goethe's fundamental concept of the 'Urphänomen'. So convinced was Goethe of the correctness of his notion of light as a unity of white, as opposed to Newton's hypothesis of light compounded of separate elements (wavelengths) which combine to appear white, that his opposition to Newton in *Zur Farbenlehre* sometimes gives the impression of a vendetta rather than a reasoned rebuttal.[32] While it may be unfair to cite Goethe in this respect, working as he was in an age before the scientific method was commonly accepted, there are enough examples in the history of science since that time to support the point. Theories of evolution, in particular, tend, ironically, to be argued with an almost religious fervour which belies the unquestioned scientific rigour of the underlying investigations.[33]

Schneider's example of the sciences, then, as an area in which error is easily admitted and theories consequently adapted or abandoned, has its flaws. And those flaws emerge in the author's use of the character of a scientist in *Paarungen*. For although Eduard is forced in the novel to admit personal error, if not any weakness in his views on heredity compared with those of the brother, his confession is hardly convincing. While in chapter 24 he declares himself guilty of 'Gemeinheiten, Halbheiten, falschen Versprechen' (*P*, 294–5), it is in the context of a complaint that guilt-feelings such as his are rarely the subject of fiction. This attack of self-pity is compounded when, finally confronted with the facts of his fatherhood by Jenny, he bemoans 'die Irrtümer der Wissenschaft' (*P*, 294), which had led him to believe that he was incapable of fathering children. On learning that he is the father of Laura's child, too, Eduard curses science itself as an inexact enterprise: 'In der Wissenschaft gab es keine unumstößlichen Wahrheiten, die einzige Konstante war die notorische Unterschätzung des Fehlerquotienten' (*P*, 295–6). The irony is that Eduard appears not to understand this himself. Even though he is willing to admit mistakes in his personal behaviour, the insight seems to have little effect on his actions. He still abandons Klara, while showing little inclination to fulfil any putative responsibility towards Laura. And there is no question of Eduard's accepting that the challenges to his research made by the protesting students and others may have some legitimate foundation. Eduard thus finally falls into the same trap for which he berates others. In the final pages of the novel he rhetorically raises the question of progress: 'Wird man nie klüger?' (*P*, 339). On the evidence of *Paarungen*, the answer, it seems, must be no.

Notes

[1] 'Wenn die Wirklichkeit die Ideen verrät' (*VEG*, 7–20) first appeared as '"Gefangen in der Geschichte". Peter Schneider über das Lagerdenken der Intellektuellen im Streit um Deutschland und den Fremdenhaß', *Der Spiegel*, 18 January 1993, 156–7, 160, 162.

² See *BP*, 210–51. First published in *Kursbuch*, 35, 1974.
³ Frankfurt am Main, Europäische Verlagsanstalt, 1966. See *BP*, 214.
⁴ For more detail on the plagiarism charge see my introduction to *Vati* (Manchester, Manchester University Press, 1993), 24–9; Gordon Burgess, '"Was da ist, das ist (nicht) mein": The Case of Peter Schneider', in Arthur Williams, Stuart Parkes and Roland Smith (eds.), *Literature on the Threshold: The German Novel in the 1980s* (Providence, Oxford and Munich, Berg, 1990), 107–22; and Peter Morgan, 'The Sins of the Fathers: A Reappraisal of the Controversy about Peter Schneider's *Vati*', *German Life and Letters*, 47 (1994), 104–33.
⁵ Iris Radisch, 'Contra', *Die Zeit*, 13 November 1992, 57.
⁶ Werner Fuld, 'Pilotfische im Stammlokal, ratlos', *Frankfurter Allgemeine Zeitung*, 31 October 1992.
⁷ At a public reading of *Paarungen* in January 1993, Schneider explained that this previously unsuspected influence on his narrative technique had been pointed out to him by a British (or American) student.
⁸ Werner Liersch noted the debt to Goethe's novel as follows: 'So hat der neue Roman in dem alten Roman einen Hintergrund, auf den sich Veränderungen der Gefühlslandschaften in einer Art verdeckten Erzählens projizieren.' See Liersch, 'Griff ins Leere. Peter Schneiders "Paarungen"', *Freitag*, 2 October 1992, 26. One other reviewer referred to the name Eduard Hoffmann as being 'freilich verziert mit ein paar Anklängen an die deutsche Klassik und Romantik'. See Leonore Schwartz, 'Eduards Freunde', *Deutsches Allgemeines Sonntagsblatt*, 4 December 1992, 30.
⁹ *Goethes Werke*, ed. Benno von Wiese and Erich Trunz (Hamburg, Christian Wegner Verlag, 1958), VI, 306, l. 33.
¹⁰ Ibid., ll. 25–7.
¹¹ Walter Benjamin, *Gesammelte Schriften*, I.I, ed. Rolf Tiedemann and Hermann Schweppenhäuser (Frankfurt am Main, Suhrkamp, 1974), I.I, 127.
¹² *Goethes Werke*, VI, 272, ll. 27–30.
¹³ Ibid., 272, ll. 39ff.
¹⁴ Ibid., 273, ll. 29–31.
¹⁵ Ibid., 274, ll. 13–18.
¹⁶ Ibid., 275, ll. 12–16.
¹⁷ While conflicts between religion and science were common in previous centuries (Galileo and Giordano Bruno being only two such cases), the ethical and political dilemmas which beset scientific enquiry in the twentieth century had yet to make their appearance.
¹⁸ Compare *MK*, 5, and *P*, 78.
¹⁹ See note 4 above.
²⁰ *V*, 64. In the passage under discussion, Schneider is paraphrasing or quoting from letters written by the historical Mengele.
²¹ For more information on this subject, see Robert Jay Lifton, *The Nazi Doctors: Medical Killing and the Psychology of Genocide* (New York, Basic Books, 1986).
²² See *DÄ*, 65–81.

[23] E. T. A. Hoffmann, *Poetische Werke*, (Berlin, Walter de Gruyter, 1957), III, 19.

[24] Ibid., 38.

[25] See Michael Schneider, 'Peter Schneider: von der Alten Radikalität zur Neuen Sensibilität', in Michael Schneider, *Die lange Wut zum langen Marsch* (Reinbek, Rowohlt, 1975), 304–34.

[26] See R. M. Gillett's essay in Chapter 7 of this volume for a fuller treatment of this story.

[27] Michael Schneider, *Das Spiegelkabinett* (Munich, AutorenEdition, 1980).

[28] Michael Schneider, 'Väter und Söhne posthum. Das beschädigte Verhältnis zweier Generationen', in Michael Schneider, *Den Kopf verkehrt aufgesetzt oder die melancholische Linke. Aspekte des Kulturzerfalls in den siebziger Jahren* (Darmstadt and Neuwied, Luchterhand, 1981), 8–64.

[29] Not as belated as it might seem, because Peter Schneider apparently began work on *Paarungen* in 1983, only three years after the publication of *Das Spiegelkabinett*.

[30] *Das Spiegelkabinett*, 55–6.

[31] 'Man kann sogar ein Erdbeben verpassen. Plädoyer für eine Vergangenheitsbewältigung der Linken', *Die Zeit*, 18 (27 April), 57–8. A longer version may be found in *EM*, 54–78.

[32] Goethe was clearly aware of the repetitive nature of his attacks on Newton. Just one example of his exasperation, as well as of the unscientific nature of his observations, may be found in his introductory assessment of Newton's work on optics in *Zur Farbenlehre*: 'Er irrt, und zwar auf eine entschiedene Weise. Erst findet er seine Theorie plausibel, dann überzeugt er sich mit Übereilung, ehe ihm deutlich wird, welcher mühseligen Kunstgriffe es bedürfen werde, die Anwendung seines hypothetischen Aperçus durch die Erfahrung durchzuführen. Aber schon hat er sie öffentlich ausgesprochen, und nun verfehlt er nicht, alle Gewandtheit seines Geistes aufzubieten, um seine These durchzusetzen; wobei er mit unglaublicher Kühnheit das ganz Absurde als ein ausgemachtes Wahre der Welt ins Angesicht behauptet'. *Goethes Werke*, XIV, 143, ll. 21–30.

[33] Whilst preparing this chapter for publication, I came across an illustration of such scientific fervour in a critique of aspects of Darwinism written for a lay audience: 'The great legal battles in the early half of the century for the right to teach American children the "anti-religious" doctrine of evolution are now long gone, and it is modern-day Darwinists who appear increasingly to function like an embattled religious order. Perhaps as a consequence, a distinctly religious cast of expression often seems to spread into their language.' Warwick Collins, 'The fatal flaw of a great theory', *The Spectator*, 31 December 1994, 7–10 (p. 7).

8

Bibliography

DUNCAN LARGE

The order of entries within each year is as follows: books and films; collaborations on books; edited journal issues; articles and interviews in books; TV programmes, and articles and interviews in journals, magazines and newspapers; articles and interviews without specific date. Titles and descriptions in square brackets have been added by the compiler.

Primary Works, 1964–1994

1964

'Über das Marat-Stück von Peter Weiß', *Neue Rundschau*, 75 No. 4, 664–72. Reprinted (as 'Peter Weiss. Die Verfolgung und Ermordung Jean Paul Marats') in Manfred Brauneck (ed.), *Das deutsche Drama vom Expressionismus bis zur Gegenwart. Interpretationen* (Bamberg, Buchner, 1970), 253–60 (2nd edn. (1972), 275–82; 3rd edn. and 4th edn. (1976), 296–303). Reprinted (as 'Über das "Marat"-Stück von Peter Weiss') in *Atempause* (1977a), 31–41.

1965

[a] 'Vom Nutzen des Klischees. Betrachtungen zum Wildwestfilm', *Sprache im technischen Zeitalter*, 13 (January–March), 1091–1107. Reprinted in *Atempause* (1977a), 42–60.

[b] 'Eine mexikanische Familie' [review of Oscar Lewis, *Die Kinder von Sánchez. Selbstporträt einer mexikanischen Familie*, tr. Margarete Bormann (Düsseldorf and Vienna, Econ-Verlag, 1963)], *Der Monat*, 197 (February), 90–1.

[c] 'Konkrete Dichtung', *Sprache im technischen Zeitalter*, 15 (July–September), 1197–214. Reprinted in Burckhard Garbe (ed.), *Konkrete Poesie, Linguistik und Sprachunterricht* (Hildesheim, Zurich and New York, Olms ('Germanistische Texte und Studien' 7), 1987), 176–95.

[d] 'Die Mängel der gegenwärtigen Literaturkritik', *Neue Deutsche Hefte*, 107 (September–October), 98–123. Reprinted in *Atempause* (1977a), 9–30.

[e] 'Die Verwüstungen durch Armut. Ein neues Buch von Oscar Lewis über das Leben zum Beispiel im Staate Mexiko' [review of Oscar Lewis, *Pedro Martinez. Selbstporträt eines Mexikaners*, tr. Margarete Bormann (Düsseldorf and Vienna, Econ-Verlag, 1965)], *Die Zeit*, 48 (26 November), V. Reprinted in *Atempause* (1977a), 63–7.

[f] 'Politische Dichtung. Ihre Grenzen und Möglichkeiten', *Der Monat*, 207 (December), 68–77. Reprinted in Peter Stein (ed.), *Theorie der Politischen Dichtung. Neunzehn Aufsätze* (Munich, Nymphenburger ('Nymphenburger Texte zur Wissenschaft. Modelluniversität' 13), 1973), 141–55.

[g] 'Hans Magnus Enzensberger, *blindenschrift*' [review of Enzensberger, *blindenschrift* (Frankfurt am Main, Suhrkamp, 1964)], *Neue Rundschau*, 76 No. 3, 510–13. Reprinted in Joachim Schickel (ed.), *Über Hans Magnus Enzensberger* (Frankfurt am Main, Suhrkamp ('Edition Suhrkamp' 403), 1970), 106–9.

1966

[a] 'Zerhackte Klaviere und andere Sachen. Eine Abrechnung mit Happening, Fluxus, Pop Art' [review of Jürgen Becker and Wolf Vostell, *Happenings, Fluxus, Pop Art, Nouveau réalisme. Eine Dokumentation* (Reinbek, Rowohlt ('Rowohlt-Paperback' 45), 1965)], *Die Zeit*, 13 (25 March), VII. Reprinted in *Atempause* (1977a), 87–100.

[b] 'Reduzierte Sprache, physische Erschöpfung. Zu sieben neuen Texten Samuel Becketts' [review of Samuel Beckett, *Aus einem aufgegebenen Werk (From an Abandoned Work) und kurze Spiele. Zweisprachig*, tr. Erika and Elmar Tophoven (Frankfurt am Main, Suhrkamp ('Edition Suhrkamp' 145), 1966)], *Die Zeit*, 20 (13 May), 28–9. Reprinted in *Atempause* (1977a), 68–73.

[c] 'Sartre als Essayist' [review of Jean-Paul Sartre, *Situationen*, tr. Werner Bökenkamp *et al.* (Reinbek, Rowohlt ('Rowohlt-Paperback' 46), 1965)], *Die Zeit*, 30 (22 July). Reprinted in *Atempause* (1977a), 78–86.

[d] 'Wäre Lyrik zur Zeit nicht aktuell? Peter Hamms Anthologie "Aussichten" und die Schwierigkeit beim Schreiben von Gedichten' [review of Peter Hamm (ed.), *Aussichten. Junge Lyriker des deutschen Sprachraums* (Munich, Biederstein, 1966)], *Die Zeit*, 39 (23 September), VI. Reprinted in *Atempause* (1977a), 101–7.

[e] 'Walter Matthias Diggelmann/*Hinterlassenschaft*' [review of Diggelmann, *Die Hinterlassenschaft. Roman* (Munich, Piper, 1965)], *Neue Rundschau*, 1966 No. 2, 315–19.

[f] 'Die Sache mit dem gelben Fleck' [review of Uwe Friesel, *Sonnenflecke. Roman* (Hamburg, Wegner, 1965)], *Sprache im technischen Zeitalter*, 17–18, 164–6.

1967

'Zurück ins Land der Geburt. Zu den Gedichten von Aimé Césaire' [review of Césaire, *Zurück ins Land der Geburt/Cahier d'un retour au pays natal*, tr. Janheinz Jalm (Frankfurt am Main, Insel, 1962)], *Die Zeit*, 33 (18 August), 14. Reprinted in *Atempause* (1977a), 74–7.

1968

[a] 'Wir haben Fehler gemacht', in Bernard Larsson (ed.), *Demonstrationen. Ein Berliner Modell. Fotos* (Berlin, Voltaire ('Voltaire Flugschriften' 10)), 158–63. Reprinted in *Ansprachen* (1970a), 7–14. Reprinted (as 'Kulturrevolution an der Universität') in Hermann L. Gremliza (ed.), *30 Jahre "Konkret"* (Hamburg, Konkret, 1987), 107–8.

[b] 'Individuelle Sachlichkeit' [review of Günter Grass, *Ausgefragt. Gedichte und Zeichnungen* (Darmstadt and Neuwied, Luchterhand, 1967)], *Kürbiskern*, 4, 169–72. Reprinted in Franz Josef Görtz (ed.), *Günter Grass. Auskunft für Leser* (Darmstadt and Neuwied, Luchterhand ('Sammlung Luchterhand' 543), 1984), 186–92.

1969

[a] *Betriebsarbeit. Untersuchungen und Protokolle* (with Marianne Herzog) (Berlin, Voltaire ('Voltaire Handbuch' 11)).

[b] 'Die Phantasie im Spätkapitalismus und die Kulturrevolution', *Kursbuch*, 16 (March), 1–37. Reprinted in *Atempause* (1977a), 127–61.
Italian: 'L'immaginazione nel tardo capitalismo e la rivoluzione culturale', tr. Lapo Berti, in *Letteratura e/o rivoluzione. Tre saggi di Kursbuch* (Milan, Feltrinelli ('Materiali' 26), 1970).

[c] 'Rede an die deutschen Leser und ihre Schriftsteller', *Kursbuch*, 16 (March), 'Kursbogen'. Reprinted in *Ansprachen* (1970a), 29–38; Renate Matthaei (ed.), *Grenzverschiebung. Neue Tendenzen in der deutschen Literatur der 60er Jahre* (Cologne, Kiepenheuer & Witsch, 1970), 'rote Seiten', 42–7; Christlieb Hirte, Heidrun Loeper, Ingeborg Quaas and Dietrich Simon (eds.), *BRD heute, Westberlin heute. Ein Lesebuch* (East Berlin, Volk und Welt, 1984), 302–9; Markus Krause and Stephan Speicher (eds.), *Absichten und Einsichten. Texte zum Selbstverständnis zeitgenössischer Autoren* (Stuttgart, Reclam, 1990), 127–35. Excerpt reprinted (as 'Kein Verkehr') in Klaus Wagenbach *et al.* (eds.), *Vaterland, Muttersprache* (see 1979b), 244–5.
French: 'Discours aux lecteurs allemands et à leurs écrivains', tr. Nicole Casanova, in *Le sable aux souliers de Baader* (see 1980a), 11–18.

[d] 'Vorbild Mao Tse-Tung', *Der Spiegel*, 15 (7 April), 177.

1970

[a] *Ansprachen. Reden, Notizen, Gedichte* (Berlin, Wagenbach ('Quarthefte' 47)); 2nd edn. (with 'Editorische Nachnotiz' by Klaus Wagenbach, 70–1), 1981. Includes:

'Reden':

[i] 'Wir haben Fehler gemacht', 7–14.

[ii] 'Die "Bild-Zeitung", ein Kampfblatt gegen die Massen', 15–28.

[iii] 'Rede an die deutschen Leser und ihre Schriftsteller', 29–38.

[iv] 'Brief an die herrschende Klasse in Deutschland', 39–42. Reprinted (as 'Peter Schneider an die herrschende Klasse in Deutschland') in Jürgen Moeller (ed.), *Historische Augenblicke. Deutsche Briefe des XX. Jahrhunderts* (Munich, Beck, 1988), 240–3.

'Notizen':

[v] 'Verdeutschung einiger Verbotsschilder', 43–4. 'Verdeutschung des Verbotsschilds: "Betreten und Befahren verboten. Privateigentum"' reprinted in *Tintenfisch*, 4 ('Quarthefte' 49, 1971), 71.

[vi] 'Unterschiede', 45.

[vii] 'Hausordnungen', 46–51.

[viii] 'Rechnung eines Hausbesitzers', 52.

[ix] 'Exemplarische Aktion eines Individuums', 53. Reprinted in *Deutsche Volkszeitung*, 45 (3 November 1989), 11.

[x] 'Entgegnung auf einige Sätze der bürgerlichen Moral', 54–5.

[xi] 'Ein subversives Element', 56.

[xii] 'Beat', 57.

[xiii] 'Subjekt–Prädikat–Objekt', 58.

[xiv] 'Straßenverkehr', 59–62. Reprinted in: *Tintenfisch*, 4 ('Quarthefte' 49, 1971), 16–18; Günter Sieber, Harald Bielig and Kurt Koszyk (eds.), *Brich auf ins Licht* (Dortmund, Hoesch, 1988), 273–5.

'Gedichte':

[xv] 'Über die Mühen des Kampfes in Deutschland', 63–5.

[xvi] 'Gift', 66–7.

[xvii] 'Rudi', 68.

[b] 'Die Frauen bei Bosch', *Kursbuch*, 21 (September), 83–109. Reprinted in *Die Botschaft des Pferdekopfs* (1981a), 59–95.
French: 'Les femmes chez Bosch', tr. Hélène Belletto, in *Le sable aux souliers de Baader* (see 1980a), 69–102.

[c] 'Brief an die herrschende Klasse in Deutschland', *Tintenfisch*, 3 ('Quarthefte' 39), 39–41. Reprinted in *Ansprachen* (1970a), 39–42.

[d] 'Rudi' [poem], *Tintenfisch*, 3 ('Quarthefte' 39), 107. Reprinted in *Ansprachen* (1970a), 68; *Freibeuter*, 3 (1980), 2–3.

1971

[a] *Kursbuch*, 26 ('Die Klassenkämpfe in Italien', December), ed. P.S.

[b] 'Bericht über eine Berliner Volksschule', *Kursbuch*, 24 (June), 61–81. Reprinted in *Die Botschaft des Pferdekopfs* (1981a), 96–125.
French: 'Rapport sur une école primaire de Berlin', tr. Hélène Belletto, in *Le sable aux souliers de Baader* (see 1980a), 151–77.

[c] 'Ratschlag zweier Deutsch-Lehrer an ihre zurückbleibenden Schüler' (with Helmut Lethen), *Kursbuch*, 24 (June), 133–53.

[d] 'Können wir aus den italienischen Klassenkämpfen lernen?', *Kursbuch*, 26 (December), 1–3. Reprinted in *Die Botschaft des Pferdekopfs* (1981a), 141–5.
French: 'Pouvons-nous tirer un enseignement des luttes de classes en Italie?', tr. Hélène Belletto, in *Le sable aux souliers de Baader* (see 1980a), 140–4.
[e] 'Die Massen, die Gewerkschaften und die politischen Avantgarden', *Kursbuch*, 26 (December), 135–62.

1972
[a] 'Protokoll einer Anhörung' ['in einer Broschüre der GEW, Berlin']. Revised version reprinted in *Die Botschaft des Pferdekopfs* (1981a), 146–57.
French: 'Procès-verbal d'une audition', tr. Hélène Belletto, in *Le sable aux souliers de Baader* (see 1980a), 178–90.
[b] 'Schulkampf' [TV documentary, with Dieter Bitterli]. First broadcast: Westdeutscher Rundfunk (Cologne), 13 December.

1973
[a] *Lenz. Eine Erzählung von 1968 und danach* (Berlin, Rotbuch ('Rotbuch' 104)). Title shortened to *Lenz. Eine Erzählung*, 1974; 2nd edn. ('Rotbuch Taschenbuch' 71), 1992. East German edn. in Annie Voigtländer (ed.), *Ein schönes Leben. Geschichten aus einer anderen Welt* (East Berlin, Neues Leben, 1977), 154–241. Book club edn. in *Lenz und andere Erzählungen* (Gütersloh, Bertelsmann-Club, n.y.). Excerpts reprinted in *Das kleine Rotbuch*, 1 (1973), 14–16; *Blickpunkt*, 235 (May 1974) (as 'Was er sagte, leuchtete ein. Leseprobe aus der Erzählung "Lenz" von Peter Schneider'); *Das kleine Rotbuch*, 11 (1983), 6; *Deutsche Volkszeitung*, 5 (31 January 1986), 13 (as 'Große Veränderungen'); *Deutsche Volkszeitung*, 30 (21 July 1989), 11; *Deutsche Volkszeitung*, 39 (22 September 1989), 11 (as 'VW-Salon').
Danish: *Lenz. En fortælling*, tr. Jørgen Bonde Jensen and Karen Nicolajsen (Viborg, Gyldendal, 1974. Samlerens Bogklub edn., 1975).
Dutch: *Lenz*, tr. Gerrit Bussink (Amsterdam, Uitgeverij De Arbeiderspers ('Grote ABC' 239), 1974).
Italian: *Lenz. Racconto*, tr. Renato Pedio (Milan, Feltrinelli ('I narratori di Feltrinelli' 235), 1975; 2nd edn. Milan, Feltrinelli economica ('Universale economica' 819), 1978).
Norwegian: *Lenz. En fortelling*, tr. Espen Haavardsholm (Oslo, Gyldendal Norsk, 1975).
Swedish: *Lenz. En berättelse*, tr. Madeleine Gústafsson (Stockholm, Pan/Norstedts, 1975).
Spanish: *Lenz. Un relato*, tr. Michael Faber-Kaiser (Barcelona, Anagrama ('Serie informal' 26), 1976; Circulo de Lectores edn. ('onda joven'), 1989).
French: *Lenz. Récit*, tr. Nicole Casanova (Paris, Flammarion ('Lettres étrangères'), 1978).

Portuguese: *Lenz. Um relato*, in Peter Schneider/Georg Büchner, *'Lenz' precedido por 'Lenz. Um relato'*, tr. Irene Aron (São Paulo, Brasiliense ('Circo de letras' 49), 1985), 7–119.
Turkish: *Lenz*, tr. Füsun Ant (Istanbul, AFA ('Çağdaş Dünya E debíyatí'), 1988).
Korean: *Lentchu* (Seoul, 1990).

[b] 'Frau Elisabeth Marquardt. Portrait eines Lebens, das in den Geschichtsbüchern nicht vorkommt' [TV documentary, with Dieter Bitterli]. First broadcast: Westdeutscher Rundfunk (Cologne), 30 June.

[c] 'Erfahrungen unter deutschen und italienischen Genossen. Drei Passagen aus der Erzählung "Lenz"', *Frankfurter Rundschau*, 233 (6 October), 8. Reprinted in (1973a).

[d] 'Lenz', *Literaturmagazin*, 1 (October), 168–75. Reprinted in (1973a), 5–16.

1974

[a] *Feuer unterm Pfauenthron. Verbotene Geschichten aus dem persischen Widerstand*, ed. and tr. Bahman Nirumand with P.S. (Berlin, Rotbuch ('Rotbuch' 124)).

[b] 'Schwierige Sexualität und Partnerschaft. Sehr subjektive Gedanken eines jungen Schriftstellers aus der Neuen Linken', *Neue Zeitung*, 11 April. Reprinted in 'Die Sache mit der "Männlichkeit"' (1974c).

[c] 'Die Sache mit der "Männlichkeit". Gibt es eine Emanzipation der Männer?', *Kursbuch*, 35 (April), 103–32. Reprinted in *Die Botschaft des Pferdekopfs* (1981a), 210–51.
French: 'La question de la virilité. Y a-t-il une émancipation des hommes?', tr. Hélène Belletto, in *Le sable aux souliers de Baader* (see 1980a), 103–39.

[d] 'Heiner Müllers *Geschichten aus der Produktion*' [review of Müller, *Geschichten aus der Produktion I* (Berlin, Rotbuch, 1974)], *Der Spiegel*, 36 (2 September), 113–27. Reprinted in *Atempause* (1977a), 177–81.

1975

[a] *. . . schon bist du ein Verfassungsfeind. Das unerwartete Anschwellen der Personalakte des Lehrers Kleff* (Berlin, Rotbuch ('Rotbuch' 140)). Excerpts reprinted in: *Pardon*, 4 (April 1976), 22–3 (as '. . . und schon bist du ein Verfassungsfeind. Notizen eines Betroffenen'); *Das kleine Rotbuch*, 3 (1975), 45–6 (as 'Das unerwartete Anschwellen der Personalakte des Lehrers Kleff'); *Tintenfisch*, 9 ('Quarthefte' 79, 1976), 91–2; *Deutsche Volkszeitung*, 12 (22 March 1979), 13; Dietrich Kayser (ed.), *Ortsbeschreibung – Autoren sehen Freiburg* (Freiburg i. Br., Rombach, 1980), 65–6; Christoph Buchwald and Klaus Wagenbach (eds.), *Lesebuch. Deutsche Literatur der siebziger Jahre* (Berlin, Wagenbach, 1984), 76–7 (as 'Die freiheitlich-demokratische').
Danish: *. . . og straks er du forfatningsfjende. Om hvordan journalen verdrørende lærer Kleff uventet voksede og voksede. En roman om det vesttyske*

Berufsverbot, tr. Jørgen Bonde Jensen and Karen Nicolajsen (Viborg, Gyldendal, 1976).
Dutch: *Een staatsvijand als jij en ik. Het onverwachte uitdijen van de konduitestaat van de leraar Kleff*, tr. Tom Graftdijk (Amsterdam, SUA, 1976) (see also 1976b).
French: *. . . te voilà un ennemi de la Constitution. Comment le dossier du professeur Kleff s'est gonflé d'une manière inattendue*, tr. Nicole Casanova (Paris, Flammarion ('Lettres étrangères'), 1976).
Swedish: *. . . och redan är du en författningsfiende. Hur lärare Kleffs personalakt plötsligt växte*, tr. Jan Nyvelius (Stockholm, Pan/Norstedts, 1976).
Italian: *Nemico della Costituzione. L'inatteso gonfiarsi del fascicolo personale dell'insegnante Kleff*, tr. Renato Pedio (Milan, Feltrinelli economica ('Universale economica' 777), 1977).
Norwegian: *. . . og straks er du en forfatningsfiende. Om hvordan arkivdokumentene angående lærer Kleff volkste og volkste*, tr. Kjell Askildsen (Oslo, Gyldendal Norsk ('Lanterne-bøkene'), 1977).
Greek: [*. . . schon bist du ein Verfassungsfeind*], 1979.
Spanish: *Ya eres un enemigo de la Constitución*, tr. Ruth Zautner (Barcelona, Montesinos ('Tundal'), 1981).
[b] 'Ein Stück in Anführungsstrichen. Gespräch mit Peter Schneider über das Radikalenerlaß-Szenarium im Kammertheater' [interview with Wolfgang Ignée], *Stuttgarter Zeitung*, 6 (9 January), 28.
[c] 'Angst aus dem Zettelkasten. Zu Peter Handke: *Die Stunde der wahren Empfindung*' [review of Handke, *Die Stunde der wahren Empfindung* (Frankfurt am Main, Suhrkamp, 1975)], *Frankfurter Rundschau*, 146 (28 June). Reprinted in *Atempause* (1977a), 187–91.
[d] 'Vom Bankräuber zum Revolutionär. Die erstaunliche Lebensgeschichte des Sante Notarnicola, von ihm selbst aufgeschrieben' [review of Sante Notarnicola, *Die Bankräuber aus der Barriera. Die Lebensgeschichte des Revolutionärs Sante Notarnicola, von ihm selbst aufgeschrieben*, tr. Peter O. Chotjewitz (Munich, Trikont ('Romane, Reportagen, Autobiographien'), 1974)], *Frankfurter Rundschau*, 293 (18 December). Reprinted in *Atempause* (1977a), 182–6.
[e] 'Biermanns neue Liebeslieder' [review of Wolf Biermann, *Liebeslieder* (CBS, 1975)], *Konkret*, 1 (December), 49. Reprinted in *Atempause* (1977a), 192–4.
[f] 'Antwort an einen anonymen Kritiker', *Langer Marsch*, 8. Reprinted in *Atempause* (1977a), 202–3.

1976

[a] 'Bier und Theater–Szenen ohne Ende mit jugendlichen Arbeitslosen', in Götz Aly, *'Wofür wirst du eigentlich bezahlt?' Möglichkeiten praktischer Erzieherarbeit zwischen Ausflippen und Anpassung* (Berlin, Rotbuch

('Rotbuch' 163)). Reprinted in *Die Botschaft des Pferdekopfs* (1981a), 126–34.

French: 'Bière et théâtre', tr. Hélène Belletto, in *Le sable aux souliers de Baader* (see 1980a), 245–59.

[b] 'Niet alleen het topje van de maatschappelijke ijsberg' [interview with Eddie Korlaar, held 30 April and 29 May, 1976], in Peter Schneider, *Een staatsvijand als jij en ik. Het onverwachte uitdijen van de konduitestaat van de leraar Kleff*, tr. Tom Graftdijk (Amsterdam, SUA, 1976), 120–30.

[c] 'Über den Unterschied von Literatur und Politik. Vortrag, gehalten in London, im Februar dieses Jahres', *Literaturmagazin*, 5 (June), 188–98. Reprinted (as 'Über den Unterschied von Literatur und Politik') in *Atempause* (1977a), 162–74.

French: 'Distinction entre littérature et politique', tr. Marie-Louise Audiberti, in *Le sable aux souliers de Baader* (see 1980a), 19–33.

[d] 'Wallraffs Arbeitsmethode' [review of Günther Wallraff, *Die Reportagen* (Cologne, Kiepenheuer & Witsch, 1976)], *Konkret*, 12 (November), 32–5. Reprinted in *Atempause* (1977a), 195–201.

[e] [Interview], *Les Nouvelles Littéraires*, 2561 (2–9 December).

[f] 'Drei Jahre danach. Frau Marquardt gewöhnt sich an das Rentnerleben' [TV documentary]. First broadcast: Westdeutscher Rundfunk (Cologne), 27 December.

[g] 'Ick hab 'nen Job für dich. Staubwischen in der Wüste' [TV programme, with Michael Geissler]. First broadcast: Westdeutscher Rundfunk (Cologne), 29 December.

1977

[a] *Atempause. Versuch, meine Gedanken über Literatur und Kunst zu ordnen* (Reinbek, Rowohlt ('das neue buch' 86)). Includes:

1: 'Standortsuche'

[i] 'Die Mängel der gegenwärtigen Literaturkritik' (9–30).

[ii] 'Über das "Marat"-Stück von Peter Weiss' (31–41).

[iii] 'Vom Nutzen des Klischees: Betrachtungen zum Wildwestfilm' (42–60).

2: 'Kritiken 1'

[iv] 'Die Verwüstungen durch Armut. Ein neues Buch von Oscar Lewis über das Leben zum Beispiel im Staate Mexiko' (63–7).

[v] 'Reduzierte Sprache, physische Erschöpfung. Zu sieben neuen Texten Samuel Becketts' (68–73).

[vi] 'Zurück ins Land der Geburt. Zu den Gedichten von Aimé Césaire' (74–7).

[vii] 'Sartre als Essayist' (78–86).

[viii] 'Zerhackte Klaviere und andere Sachen. Eine Abrechnung mit Happening, Fluxus, Pop Art' (87–100).

[ix] 'Wäre Lyrik zur Zeit nicht aktuell? Peter Hamms Anthologie "Aussichten" und die Schwierigkeit beim Schreiben von Gedichten' (101–7).
3: 'Politik und Literatur'
[x] 'Literatur als Widerstand. Am Beispiel von Bert Brechts *Arturo Ui*' (111–25).
[xi] 'Die Phantasie im Spätkapitalismus und die Kulturrevolution' (127–61).
[xii] 'Über den Unterschied von Literatur und Politik' (162–74).
4: 'Kritiken 2'
[xiii] 'Heiner Müllers *Geschichten aus der Produktion*' (177–81).
[xiv] 'Vom Bankräuber zum Revolutionär. Die erstaunliche Lebensgeschichte des Sante Notarnicola, von ihm selbst aufgeschrieben' (182–6).
[xv] 'Angst aus dem Zettelkasten. Zu Peter Handke: *Die Stunde der wahren Empfindung*' (187–91).
[xvi] 'Biermanns neue Liebeslieder' (192–4).
[xvii] 'Wallraffs Arbeitsmethode' (195–201).
[xviii] 'Antwort an einen anonymen Kritiker' (202–3).
5: 'Nachwort'
[xix] 'Die Beseitigung der ersten Klarheit' (207–35).
French: 'Suppression de la clarté première', tr. Marie-Louise Audiberti, in *Le sable aux souliers de Baader* (see 1980a), 263–93.
[b] 'Peter Schneider zur Unterschrift der Professoren unter die Erklärung des Ministers Pestel', in Heiner Boehncke and Dieter Richter (eds.), *Nicht heimlich und nicht kühl. Entgegnungen an Dienst- und andere Herren* (Berlin, Ästhetik und Kommunikation), 28–9.
French: 'En introduction: Professeur Eduard Pestel', tr. Hélène Belletto, in *Le sable aux souliers de Baader* (see 1980a), 191–4.
[c] 'Die Ballade vom armen Bruno S. Peter Schneider über Werner Herzogs neuen Film "Stroszek"', *Der Spiegel*, 24 (6 June), 195–7.
[d] '"Nicht der Egoismus verfälscht das politische Engagement, sondern der Versuch, ihn zu verheimlichen". Beim Durchlesen früherer Aufsätze vergangene Eindrücke vergegenwärtigen', *Frankfurter Rundschau*, 144 (25 June), 3. Reprinted (as part of 'Die Beseitigung der ersten Klarheit') in *Atempause* (1977a).
[e] 'Erster Auftritt einer neuen Protest-Generation', *Pflasterstrand*. Reprinted in *Die Botschaft des Pferdekopfs* (1981a), 135–40.

1978

[a] *Die Wette. Erzählungen* (Berlin, Rotbuch ('Rotbuch' 186)). Book club edn. in *Lenz und andere Erzählungen* (Gütersloh, Bertelsmann-Club, n.y.). Includes:

[i] 'Das Ende jeder Diskussion' (7–22). Reprinted in Stephan Wantzen (ed.), *Um die Ecke Gehen. Ein literarisches Lesebuch* (Berlin, Rotbuch, 1993), 134–47. Excerpt reprinted in *Das kleine Rotbuch*, 6 (1978), 27–8.

[ii] 'Zeit zum Sterben' (23–32).

[iii] 'Die Wette' (33–46).

[iv] 'Experiment mit mehreren Männern' (47–64).

[v] 'Verloren im dritten Satz' (65–76).

[vi] 'Der große und der kleine Bruder' (77–97).

[vii] 'Das Wiedersehen' (98–111). Reprinted in Manfred Durzak (ed.), *Erzählte Zeit. 50 deutsche Kurzgeschichten der Gegenwart* (Stuttgart, Reclam, 1980), 403–14.

[b] *Messer im Kopf* [film], dir. Reinhard Hauff. Munich, Biskop-Film, Hallelujah-Film; Cologne, Westdeutscher Rundfunk. First nights: 6 October (France, Paris); 27 October (Germany, Hof). Screenplay published as *Messer im Kopf. Drehbuch* (1979a).

[c] 'Alte und neue Szenen zum Thema "Radikale"' (with the Ensemble des Württembergischen Staatstheaters and the Arbeitskreis Theater Frankfurt), in Sozialistisches Büro, Offenbach (ed.), *Theaterstücke zum Radikalenerlaß. Texte, Bilder und Dokumente* (Offenbach, Verlag 2000 ('Politisches Theater')), 15–65.
First performed (as *Geschäftszeichen I A a 5. Alte und neue Szenen zum Thema 'Radikale'*): Stuttgart, Kammertheater, 16 January 1975 (dir. Alfred Kirchner).

[d] 'Rede vor dem Russell-Tribunal', in Deutscher Beirat und Sekretariat des 3. internationalen Russell-Tribunals (ed.), *3. Internationales Russell-Tribunal. Zur Situation der Menschenrechte in der Bundesrepublik Deutschland. Bd 1: Dokumente, Verhandlungen, Ergebnisse* (Berlin, Rotbuch ('Rotbuch' 185)). Reprinted in *Die Botschaft des Pferdekopfs* (1981a), 158–74.
French: 'La pratique des auditions. Rapport présenté au tribunal Russel [*sic*]', tr. Hélène Belletto, in *Le sable aux souliers de Baader* (see 1980a), 195–211.

[e] 'Der Sand an Baaders Schuhen', *Kursbuch*, 51 (March), 1–15. Reprinted in *Die Botschaft des Pferdekopfs* (1981a), 188–209.
French: 'Et ce sable aux chaussures de Baader . . .', tr. Annie Golden and Christine Bazetou, *Les Temps Modernes*, 35 No. 396–7 ('Allemagne fédérale: difficile démocratie', July–August 1979), 318–31; 'Le sable aux souliers de Baader', tr. Hélène Belletto, in *Le sable aux souliers de Baader* (see 1980a), 224–44.

[f] '"Eine Schande für jeden unbescholtenen Bürger". Der Schriftsteller Peter Schneider sprach vor dem Russell-Tribunal zur Praxis der "Anhörung" von Lehramtsbewerbern', *Frankfurter Rundschau*, 98 (11 May), 14–15.
Longer version reprinted as 'Rede vor dem Russell-Tribunal' (1978d).

[g] 'Gespräch mit Peter Schneider' [interview on *Atempause* with Jos

Hoogeveen, Gerd Labroisse and Dick van Stekelenburg, held March 1977], *Deutsche Bücher*, 8 No. 4, 249–60.

1979

[a] *Messer im Kopf. Drehbuch* (Berlin, Rotbuch ('Rotbuch' 208)). Excerpts reprinted in: *Berliner Hefte*, 10 (1979), 97–102 (as 'Messer im Kopf. Aus dem Drehbuch'); *Das kleine Rotbuch*, 7 (1979), 51–2. Film: *Messer im Kopf* (1978b).
French: *Le couteau dans la tête. Scénario*, tr. Nicole Casanova (Paris, Hachette ('Bibliothèque allemande'), 1979).
Italian: *Il coltello in testa. Sceneggiatura del film*, tr. Renato Pedio (Milan, Feltrinelli economica ('Universale economica' 902), 1980).

[b] Two 'Slogans' and 'Standardrede' (for the 'Wahlkontor deutscher Schriftsteller', 1965), 'Kein Verkehr' and 'Ein Gedächtnisprotokoll', in Klaus Wagenbach, Winfried Stephan and Michael Krüger (eds.), *Vaterland, Muttersprache. Deutsche Schriftsteller und ihr Staat seit 1945* (Berlin, Wagenbach ('Quarthefte' 100)), 230, 231, 244–5, 293–4. 2nd edn. (ed. Klaus Wagenbach, Winfried Stephan, Michael Krüger and Susanne Schüssler), 1994.

[c] 'L'an 01 de la mémoire' [interview on *Messer im Kopf* with Nicole Casanova], *Les Nouvelles Littéraires*, 2677 (8–15 March), 12.

[d] 'Georg Büchner. *Lenz–Der hessische Landbote*' [review of Büchner, *Lenz–Der hessische Landbote* (Stuttgart, Reclam, 1979)], *Die Zeit*, 29 (13 July), 34. Revised version reprinted (as 'Georg Büchner. *Lenz*') in Fritz J. Raddatz (ed.), *ZEIT-Bibliothek der 100 Bücher* (Frankfurt am Main, Suhrkamp ('Suhrkamp Taschenbuch' 645), 1980), 193–8.

1980

[a] 'Le Convegno de Bologne', tr. Marie-Louise Audiberti, in *Le sable aux souliers de Baader*, tr. Marie-Louise Audiberti, Hélène Belletto and Nicole Casanova (Paris, P.O.L. Hachette ('Bibliothèque allemande')), 145–50.

[b] 'Der verfolgte Verfolger Franz Josef Strauß' ['Auszug aus einem Radioessay von 1967'], in Heinar Kipphardt (ed.), *Aus Liebe zu Deutschland. Satiren zu Franz Josef Strauß* (Munich, AutorenEdition), 113–25.
French: 'Le persécuteur persécuté, Franz Josef Strauss', tr. Marie-Louise Audiberti, in *Le sable aux souliers de Baader* (see 1980a), 35–68.

[c] 'Mythen des deutschen Alltags. Über Thomas Brasch, "Der schöne 27. September"', *Der Spiegel*, 18 (28 April), 244–7. Reprinted (as 'Mythen des deutschen Alltags') in Margarete Häßel and Richard Weber (eds.), *Arbeitsbuch Thomas Brasch* (Frankfurt am Main, Suhrkamp ('Suhrkamp Taschenbuch Materialien' 2076), 1987), 215–20.

1981

[a] *Die Botschaft des Pferdekopfs und andere Essais aus einem friedlichen Jahrzehnt* (Darmstadt and Neuwied, Luchterhand ('Sammlung Luchterhand' 370)). Includes:
I: 'Die Botschaft des Pferdekopfs'
[i] 'Die Botschaft des Pferdekopfs', 7–58. Excerpt reprinted in *Totoloque. Das Geiseldrama von Mexiko-Tenochtitlán. Stück in drei Spielen* [programme] (Munich, Bayerisches Staatsschauspielhaus, June 1985), 5–7.
Italian: excerpts published as 'Il messagio della testa di cavallo', tr. Carla Coccia, *Altri Termini*, 1 (June–September 1983), 23–8.
II: 'Wege nach Innen'
[ii] 'Die Frauen bei Bosch', 59–95.
[iii] 'Bericht über eine Berliner Volksschule', 96–125.
[iv] 'Bier und Theater–Szenen ohne Ende mit jugendlichen Arbeitslosen', 126–34.
[v] 'Erster Auftritt einer neuen Protest-Generation', 135–40.
[vi] 'Können wir aus den italienischen Klassenkämpfen lernen?', 141–5.
III: 'Das Ohr des Staates'
[vii] 'Protokoll einer Anhörung', 146–57.
[viii] 'Rede vor dem Russell-Tribunal', 158–74.
IV: 'Der Zweikampf'
[ix] 'Die Widersprüche der Justiz', 175–87 ('wurde 1973 für den *Spiegel* geschrieben und dort nicht veröffentlicht').
[x] 'Der Sand an Baaders Schuhen', 188–209.
V: 'Die Sache mit der "Männlichkeit". Gibt es eine Emanzipation der Männer?'
[xi] 'Die Sache mit der "Männlichkeit". Gibt es eine Emanzipation der Männer?', 210–51.
[b] 'Verweigerung ist nicht genug' [interview with Gerhard Bott], in Eberhard Knödler-Bunte (ed.), *Was ist heute noch links?* (Berlin, Ästhetik und Kommunikation ('Ästhetik und Kommunikation: Akut' 6)).
[c] 'Mit Goethe durch Latein-Amerika. Ein ZEIT-Gespräch mit Peter Schneider. Ein deutscher Schriftsteller berichtet über seine Erfahrungen bei einer Reise durch fünf Länder Latein-Amerikas' [interview with Fritz J. Raddatz], *Die Zeit*, 21 (15 May), 16.
[d] 'Aufgegebenes Gelände', *Freibeuter*, 8 ('20 Jahre Mauer'), 55–62. Excerpt reprinted in Roland Jerzewski (ed.), *Literarische Texte zur deutschen Frage nach 1945* (Berlin and Munich, Langenscheidt ('Literatur und Landeskunde' 1), 1986), 12–14.
Swedish: 'Uppgiven terräng', tr. Fredrik Sjörgren, *ord&bild*, 1982 No. 3 ('Ett nytt Europa'), 3–11.
[e] 'Die Botschaft des Pferdekopfs. Eine brasilianische Reise von Peter Schneider', *Trans Atlantik*, 5, 28–39. Longer version reprinted in *Die Botschaft des Pferdekopfs* (1981a), 7–58.

1982

[a] *Der Mann auf der Mauer. Mit Materialien zum Film von Reinhard Hauff* (Darmstadt and Neuwied, Luchterhand ('Sammlung Luchterhand' 433)).

[b] *Der Mauerspringer. Erzählung* (Darmstadt and Neuwied, Luchterhand (1984: 'Sammlung Luchterhand' 472); 1991 (Munich, dtv): 'Sammlung Luchterhand im dtv' 61472). Deutsche Buchgesellschaft edn., 1984. Film: *Der Mann auf der Mauer*, 1982. Excerpts reprinted in: *die tageszeitung*, 744 (25 March 1982), 14–16 (as 'Lena'); Jürgen Liebing (ed.), *Heimat deine Heimat. Ein Lesebuch* (Darmstadt and Neuwied, Luchterhand ('Sammlung Luchterhand' 400), 1982), 121–2 (as 'Doppelte Heimat'); Ingrid Krüger and Eike Schmitz (eds.), *Berlin, du deutsche deutsche Frau. Eine literarische Chronik der geteilten Stadt* (Darmstadt and Neuwied, Luchterhand ('Sammlung Luchterhand Bildbuch' 509), 1985), 13–14 (as 'Das Wetter wird in Berlin. . . '), 56 (as 'Als ich nach Berlin zog . . .'), 148–50 (as 'Der Bahnsteig am Stuttgarter Platz . . .'), 163–6 (as 'Ich lebe seit zwanzig Jahren in der siamesischen Stadt'); Per Ketman (ed.), *Geh doch rüber! Begegnungen von Menschen aus Ost und West. Ein Lesebuch* (Darmstadt and Neuwied, Luchterhand, 1986), 139–42 (as 'Robert'); Roland Jerzewski (ed.), *Literarische Texte zur deutschen Frage nach 1945* (Berlin and Munich, Langenscheidt ('Literatur und Landeskunde' 1), 1986), 17–20 (as 'Die Geschichte von den drei Kinogängern'), 25–7 (as 'Die Mauer im Kopf'), 32–3 (as 'Die deutsche Frage hat Speck angesetzt'); Barbara and Walter Laufenberg (eds.), *Reise Textbuch Berlin. Ein literarischer Begleiter auf den Wegen durch die Stadt* (Munich, dtv, 1987), 30 (as 'Seit gestern tausend Jahre vergangen'); *Deutsche Volkszeitung*, 28 (7 July 1989), 11.

Danish: *Murspringeren*, tr. Niels Brunse (Viborg, Gyldendal, 1983).

Dutch: *De man op de muur*, tr. W. Wielek-Berg (Amsterdam, Wereld-bibliotheek, 1983).

English: *The Wall Jumper*, tr. Leigh Hafrey (New York, Pantheon, 1983 (1985 paperback edn. as *The Wall Jumper: A Berlin Story*); London, Allison & Busby, 1984).

Finnish: *Muurinylittäjä*, tr. Markku Mannila (Helsinki, Otava, 1983).

French: *Le sauteur de mur. Récit*, tr. Nicole Casanova (Paris, Grasset, 1983). Excerpt printed (as 'L'homme sur le mur') in Klaus Schuffels (ed.), *Berlin. Le ciel partagé* (Paris, Autrement ('Série monde' 1), 1983), 14–16 (see also 1983a).

Norwegian: *Over muren*, tr. Peter Magnus (Oslo, Gyldendal Norsk, 1983).

Japanese: [*Der Mauerspringer*], tr. Kazuhiro Ochi (Tokyo, Hakusuisha, 1984).

Swedish: *Murhopparen*, tr. Eva Liljegren (Stockholm, Bonniers, 1984).

Portuguese: *Os saltadores do muro. Romance*, tr. Reinaldo Guarany (São Paulo, Marco Zero, 1986).

Hebrew: [*Der Mauerspringer*], (Ramat-Gan, Kinneret, 1987).

Portuguese (II): *O Saltador do Muro. Romance*, tr. Ana Maria Ary and Santos Damiño (Lisbon, Cotovia, 1989).
Spanish: *El Saltador del muro*, tr. Juan J. del Solar (Barcelona, Anagrama, 1985; 2nd edn. ('Panorama de narrativas'), 1989).
Italian: *Il Saltatore del muro. Romanzo*, tr. (and intro.) Lidia Castellani (Milan, SugarCo, 1991). Excerpt published (as 'Berlino città immaginaria', tr. Anita Raja) in *MicroMega*, 1986 No. 3 (July–September 1986), 175–85.

[c] *Niemands Land* (with photographs by Monika Hasse) (Berlin, Frölich & Kaufmann). Includes (P.S.): 'Der Letzte macht das Licht aus' and 'Das Vergehen der Zeit fotografieren. Beschreibung einer Methode'.

[d] 'Etwas griff nach ihm' ['Textfragment, entstanden im Zusammenhang mit dem Drehbuch *Messer im Kopf*'], *Das kleine Rotbuch*, 10 (1982), 52–3.

[e] 'Vier deutsche Schriftsteller, die in Berlin leben, rufen zum Frieden auf' [open letter ('West-Berlin, 17. April 1980') from Thomas Brasch, Günter Grass, Sarah Kirsch and P.S.: 'An die Bundesregierung der Bundesrepublik Deutschland. Zu Händen Herrn Bundeskanzler Helmut Schmidt'], in Ingrid Krüger (ed.), *Mut zur Angst. Schriftsteller für den Frieden* (Darmstadt and Neuwied, Luchterhand), 18–19. Reprinted in Günter Grass, *Widerstand lernen. Politische Gegenreden 1980–1983* (Darmstadt and Neuwied, Luchterhand ('Sammlung Luchterhand' 555), 1984), 13–14. Reprinted (as 'An die Regierung der Bundesrepublik Deutschland') in Klaus Wagenbach *et al.* (eds.), *Vaterland, Muttersprache* (see 1979b), 2nd edn. (1994), 325.

[f] [Interventions], in *Berliner Begegnung zur Friedensförderung. Protokolle des Schriftstellertreffens am 13./14. Dezember 1981* (Darmstadt and Neuwied, Luchterhand, 1982), 72–4, 141.

[g] 'Geschichte einer Trennung', *Frankfurter Rundschau*, 8 May, 111. Reprinted in *Deutsche Ängste* (1988a), 19–29.

[h] 'Warnung vor diesem Frieden', *Kursbuch*, 68 (June), 180–7. Reprinted in *Deutsche Ängste* (1988a), 30–40.

[i] 'Was den Sinn von Leben wirklich ausmacht, kann das Wort "Frieden" niemals definieren' [interview with Jürgen Holwein and Joe Bauer], *Stuttgarter Nachrichten*, 230 (6 October), Literaturbeilage, 1.

1983

[a] [Interventions], in 'Des parpaings dans la tête' [round-table discussion between Hans-Christoph Buch, P.S., Hans-Joachim Schädlich and Klaus Schlesinger], tr. Sabine Cornille, in Klaus Schuffels (ed.), *Berlin. Le ciel partagé* (Paris, Autrement ('Série monde' 1), 1983), 17–24 (P.S., 18–24).

[b] [Interventions], in *Zweiter Berliner Begegnung. Den Frieden erklären. Protokolle des Zweiten Berliner Schriftstellertreffens am 22./23. April 1983* (Darmstadt and Neuwied, Luchterhand ('Sammlung Luchterhand' 503)), 11–12, 37–9, 68–9, 78–9, 112–13, 123, 144–6, 152. Excerpt (68–9) reprinted

120   *Duncan Large*

in Klaus Wagenbach *et al.* (eds.), *Vaterland, Muttersprache* (see 1979b), 2nd edn. (1994), 348–9.

[c] '"Mit starrem Blick auf die Raketen"' [interview with Christa Schmidt], *die tageszeitung*, 25 April, 3.

[d] 'Berlin, prison dorée. Un entretien avec Peter Schneider' [interview with Philippe Boyer], *Le Nouvel Observateur*, 26 August, 58–60.

[e] 'Keine Lust aufs grüne Paradies', *Der Spiegel*, 47 (21 November), 56–7. Longer version reprinted in: *Kursbuch*, 74 (December 1983), 180–8; *Deutsche Ängste* (1988a), 41–53. Excerpt reprinted in Klaus Wagenbach *et al.* (eds.), *Vaterland, Muttersprache* (see 1979b), 2nd edn. (1994), 360–1. Italian: 'Contro la mistica del pacifismo', *Tempo illustrato*, December 1983. Reprinted (as 'I paradisi verdi') in Jürgen Humburg (ed.), *Il pensiero verde* (Bologna, il lavoro editoriale, 1986), 83–94.

[f] ['Drei Gedichte'], *Jahresring*, 30 (1983–84), 116–18. Includes: 'Mythen der neuen Welt' (116–17). Reprinted in: *drehpunkt*, 17 No. 63 (October 1985), 10–11; *L 80*, 36 (1985), 10. 'Nowhere Man' (117–18). Reprinted in Abteilung Literatur der Akademie der Künste (ed.), *Berliner Autoren–Stadtbuch* (Berlin, Akademie der Künste ('Schriftenreihe der Akademie der Künste' 17), 1985), 170. 'Klage eines tief verstörten Hausbesitzers' (118).

[g] 'Rencontre avec Peter Schneider' [interview with Odile Vassas and Gérard Fons, held 7 and 24 April 1983], *Le hangar éphémère*, 4 (1983), 114–32.

1984

[a] 'Peter Schneider. La langue allemande est sa patrie' [interview with Daniel Rondeau, held 19 May 1983], in Daniel Rondeau (ed.), *Trans-Europ-Express. Un an de reportage littéraire à 'Libération'* (Paris, Seuil), 79–85.
German: 'Peter Schneider. Die Muttersprache als Vaterland', in Daniel Rondeau (ed.), *Trans-Europ-Express. Literarische Reportagen und Interviews*, tr. Ulrich Hartmann (Freiburg i.Br., Beck und Glückler, 1985), 58–64.

[b] 'Plädoyer für einen "Verräter". Schriftsteller Peter Schneider über den Ex-Terroristen Peter-Jürgen Boock', *Der Spiegel*, 7 (13 February), 66, 68–9.

1985

[a] *Totoloque. Das Geiseldrama von Mexiko-Tenochtitlán. Stück in drei Spielen* (Darmstadt and Neuwied, Luchterhand (1989: 'Sammlung Luchterhand' 847)).
Radio version first broadcast: Sender Freies Berlin, Südwestfunk (Stuttgart) and Westdeutscher Rundfunk (Cologne), 1 June 1985.
Stage version first performed: Munich, Residenztheater, 4 July 1985 (dir. Wilfried Minks).

[b] *Ratte – tot . . . Ein Briefwechsel* (with Peter-Jürgen Boock) (Darmstadt and Neuwied, Luchterhand ('Sammlung Luchterhand' 575)). Includes (P.S.):

'Gespräche eines Schiffbrüchigen mit einem Bewohner des Festlands' (6–17).
Danish: *Rotte – Død . . . En brevveksling*, tr. Hans Christian Fink (Copenhagen, politisk revy, 1986).
[c] 'Peter Schneider', in Jean-François Fogel and Daniel Rondeau (eds.), *Pourquoi écrivez-vous? 400 écrivains répondent* (Paris, SNPC/Libération), 338–9. 2nd edn. Livre de poche ('biblio essais' 4086), 1988.
[d] 'Gespräche eines Schiffbrüchigen mit einem Bewohner des Festlands', *Die Zeit*, 15 (5 April). Reprinted in *Ratte – tot . . .* (1985b), 6–17.
[e] 'In China, hinter der Mauer. Bericht über eine Reise ins Land der zarten Gesten und der unbestimmten Blicke', *Die Zeit*, 26 (21 June), 39–40.
[f] 'Antwort an Petrarcas Freund' [poem], *drehpunkt*, 17 No. 63 (October 1985), 11. Reprinted in: *L 80*, 36 (1985), 11; Christoph Buchwald and Elke Erb (eds.), *Luchterhand Jahrbuch der Lyrik 1986. Jetzt. In unserer Lage* (Darmstadt and Neuwied, Luchterhand, 1986), 83.
[g] 'Über das allmähliche Verschwinden einer Himmelsrichtung. Variationen über das Thema "Der Intellektuelle und die Macht"' ['die überarbeitete Fassung eines Vortrags, den Peter Schneider im Oktober 1984 in Athen auf dem Kongreß "Der Schriftsteller und die Macht" hielt'], *Literaturmagazin*, 16 (October), 48–59. Reprinted (as 'Über das allmähliche Verschwinden einer Himmelsrichtung') in *Deutsche Ängste* (1988a), 54–64.
[h] '"Dir müßte man einen Orden geben". Schriftsteller Peter Schneider über eine Begegnung mit Pier Paolo Pasolinis Mörder', *Der Spiegel*, 48 (25 November), 238–9, 242, 244, 246–7, 249, 251.

1986
[a] 'Deutsche Autoren heute, 7. Peter Schneider' [taped interview with Helmut Pfeiffer, held 12 October 1984]. Bonn, Inter Nationes.
[b] 'Up Against It: The Berlin Wall, Concrete Symbol of the Divided Self', tr. Joel Agee, *Harper's Magazine*, 273 No. 1635 (August), 47–53.
[c] 'Bestätigung der Betonköpfe. Peter Schneider über den Hintergrund der Verurteilung Jürgen [sic] Boocks', *die tageszeitung*, 29 November.
[d] 'Peter Schneider' [response to question: 'Hat die Hoffnung noch eine Zukunft?'], *Die Zeit*, 1987 No. 1 (26 December), 31.

1987
[a] *Das Ende der Befangenheit?* (Paderborn, Rektor der Universität ('Paderborner Universitätsreden' 12)). Reprinted in *Deutsche Ängste* (1988a), 65–81. Excerpt reproduced (in typescript facsimile) in Hartmut Steinecke (ed.), *Literarisches aus erster Hand* (see 1994c), 112–13.
English: 'Hitler's Shadow: On Being a Self-Conscious German', tr. Leigh Hafrey, *Harper's Magazine*, 275 No. 1648 (September 1987), 49–54.
[b] *Vati. Erzählung* (Darmstadt and Neuwied, Luchterhand (1989: 'Sammlung Luchterhand' 847); 1989 (Munich, dtv): 'Sammlung

Luchterhand im dtv' 61847). Ed. (with intro. and notes) Colin Riordan as *Peter Schneider: Vati* (Manchester, Manchester University Press ('Manchester German Texts'); New York, St Martin's Press, 1993) (see also 1993a). Excerpt reprinted (as 'Wutz, Wutz, der Wutz hat es getan') in *Deutsche Volkszeitung*, 21 (22 May 1987), 13.

French: *Cet homme-là*, tr. Patrice Van Eersel (Paris, Grasset, 1988).

Italian: *Papà*, tr. (and postface) Simonetta D'Alessandro (Rome, E/O, 1988).

Portuguese: *Papá*, tr. Artur Lopes Cardoso (Lisbon, edições 70 ('Caligrafias' 6), 1988).

Swedish: *Pappa*, tr. Eva Liljegren (Stockholm, Bonniers, 1988).

Catalan: *Papa*, tr. Lourdes Bigorra (Barcelona, Magrana ('Meridiana' 3), 1989).

Welsh: excerpt ('Vati (Peter Schneider)') tr. Mererid Hopwood, *Barn*, 371–2 (December 1993–January 1994), 65–7.

[c] 'Berlin, Berlin', in Manfred Bissinger (ed.), *Auskunft über Deutschland* (Hamburg and Zurich, Rasch und Röhring), 242–56.

[d] 'Von der "beidseitig-einseitigen Abrüstung"' ['Beitrag zur Diskussion während der Zweiten Heilbronner Begegnung 1985'], in Dagmar Bruckmann, Elisabeth Hackenbracht, Alfred and Susanne Huber (eds.), *Beharrlich erinnern. Texte zur Heilbronner Begegnung* (Neckarsulm and Munich, Jungjohann), 59–62.

[e] 'Fragen an die Ausländer-raus-Deutschen. Anläßlich der Selbstverbrennung einer Türkin in Hamburg' [poem], in *Beharrlich erinnern* (see 1987d), 178–9.

[f] 'Berlino Ovest: una prigione molto comoda. Intervista a Peter Schneider' [interview with Sandro Pirovano, held December 1986], in Sandro Pirovano, *Berlino* (Milan, Clup), 7–16; 2nd edn. (Milan, CittàStudi ('Clup-Guide'), 1991), 17–26.

[g] 'Lost Innocents: The Myth of Missing Children', tr. Joel Agee, *Harper's Magazine*, 274 No. 1641 (February), 47–53. Original version published as 'Im Land der guten Onkel. Eine Erzählung aus Kalifornien', *Die Zeit*, 1 (1 January 1988), 52.

[h] 'Ist "Vati" Mengele geschützt? Der Erzähler Peter Schneider und das Copyright', *Frankfurter Rundschau*, 65 (18 March), 17.

[i] 'Im Todeskreis der Schuld', *Die Zeit*, 14 (27 March), 65–6. Longer revised version reprinted as *Das Ende der Befangenheit*? (1987a).

French: 'Le cercle infernal de la faute', tr. Anne-Lise Stern, *Les Temps Modernes*, 42 No. 495 (October 1987), 86–99.

[j] 'Coping with the Darkest Chapter of History', *New York Times*, 13 September, Section 4, 4. Longer original version published as 'Vom richtigen Umgang mit dem Bösen' in *Deutsche Ängste* (1988a), 82–121.

[k] 'My American Biography: Peter Schneider reflects on America/Meine amerikanische Biographie. Peter Schneider reflektiert über Amerika',

Ricochet, 1 (Autumn), 21–9. Excerpt reprinted (as 'Meine amerikanische Biographie (Auszug)') in *Litfass*, 13 No. 47 (November 1989), 97–9.

[l] 'Berliner Geschichten', *Natur*, 9. Reprinted in *Deutsche Ängste* (1988a), 6–18.

1988

[a] *Deutsche Ängste. Sieben Essays* (Darmstadt, Luchterhand ('Sammlung Luchterhand' 782); 1988 (Munich, dtv): 'Sammlung Luchterhand im dtv' 61782). Includes:
[i] 'Berliner Geschichten' (6–18).
[ii] 'Geschichte einer Trennung' (19–29).
[iii] 'Warnung vor diesem Frieden' (30–40).
[iv] 'Keine Lust aufs grüne Paradies' (41–53).
[v] 'Über das allmähliche Verschwinden einer Himmelsrichtung' (54–64).
[vi] 'Das Ende der Befangenheit?' (65–81).
[vii] 'Vom richtigen Umgang mit dem Bösen' (82–121).

[b] *Leyla und Medjnun. Märchen für Musik* (with Aras Ören) [libretto], 1. Münchner Biennale. Full version published Berlin, Babel Verlag Hund und Toker ('Berliner Edition'), 1992.

[c] 'Das Licht am Ende des Erzählens', in Heinz Ludwig Arnold (ed.), *Bestandsaufnahme Gegenwartsliteratur. Bundesrepublik Deutschland, Deutsche Demokratische Republik, Österreich, Schweiz* (Munich, text + kritik), 54–60. English: 'The Light at the End of the Novel', tr. Leigh Hafrey, *New York Times Book Review*, 26 July 1987, 3, 23, 25.

[d] 'Lob des Zweifels', *Frankfurter Rundschau*, 4 June, 'Zeit und Bild', 3. Longer versioin reprinted as 'Plädoyer für eine Kultur des Zweifelns' (1988e).

[e] 'Plädoyer für eine Kultur des Zweifelns', *Literaturmagazin*, 22 (September), 14–24. Reprinted in Paul Michael Lützeler (ed.), *Hoffnung Europa. Deutsche Essays von Novalis bis Enzensberger* (Frankfurt am Main, Fischer, 1994). Excerpt reprinted (as 'Über das allmähliche Verschwinden einer Himmelsrichtung') in *Ein Traum von Europa. Schriftsteller laden Schriftsteller ein* (Kongresszeitung, Berliner Kongresshalle, 25–29 May 1988), 8.
English: 'Is There a Europe? After Empire, Yalta, and Malaise', tr. Leigh Hafrey, *Harper's Magazine*, 277 No. 1660 (September 1988), 55–9.
French: 'Plaidoyer pour une culture du doute', tr. Danielle Renon, *Cosmopolitiques*, 8 (October 1988), 55–65.

1989

[a] 'Peter Schneider' [interview], in Uwe Prell and Lothar Wilker (eds.), *Die Freie Universität Berlin 1948–1968–1988. Ansichten und Einsichten* (Berlin, Arno Spitz), 187–95.

[b] 'Von Begeisterung bis Brechreiz. Eine Zeitungskritik', in *TAZ-Sonderheft zum zehnjährigen Bestehen* (Berlin, die tageszeitung), 40–4.

[c] 'A New Breed at the Barricades' [review of H. Stuart Hughes, *Sophisticated Rebels: The Political Culture of European Dissent, 1968–1987* (Cambridge, MA, Harvard University Press, 1988)], tr. Krishna Winston, *New York Times Book Review*, 8 January, 8.

[d] 'If the Wall Came Tumbling Down: Ironically, the two Germanys would lose the only thing still unifying them', tr. Krishna Winston, *New York Times Magazine*, 25 June, 22–4, 26–7, 61–2, 65, 70. Original version published as 'Was wäre, wenn die Mauer fällt', *die tageszeitung*, 2960 (14 November), 13–14; reprinted with minor revisions in *Extreme Mittellage* (1990a), 157–76.

French:'Le mur dans la tête. Et s'il tombait? Réponses avant et après le 9 novembre', in Vincent Jauvert (ed.), *Berlin. Le jour où le monde a changé* (Paris, Le Nouvel Observateur ('Documents Observateur' 8), 1990), 13–23.

[f] 'For a Berlin Novelist, the Plot Has Changed' [interview with Richard Bernstein], *New York Times*, 14 November, 20.

[g] 'Der 9. November 1989, aus 10 000 km Entfernung betrachtet', *die tageszeitung*, 2960 (14 November). Reprinted in *Extreme Mittellage* (1990a), 9–12.

[h] 'He Sees One People, But Two Germanies' [interview], *New York Newsday*, 29 November, 61, 64.

1990

[a] *Extreme Mittellage. Eine Reise durch das deutsche Nationalgefühl* (Reinbek, Rowohlt; 2nd edn. ('rororo Sachbuch' 8718), 1992). Includes:

[i] 'Vorrede' (1st edn. only: 7–8).

[ii] 'Der 9. November 1989, aus 10 000 km Entfernung betrachtet' (9–12; 2nd edn., 13–16).

[iii] 'West-Östliche Passagen' (13–32; 2nd edn., 17–33).

[iv] 'Reise durch das deutsche Nationalgefühl' (33–53; 2nd edn., 34–51).

[v] 'Man kann sogar ein Erdbeben verpassen' (54–78; 2nd edn., 52–74).

[vi] '"In Deutschland hat Saigon gesiegt". Vietnamesen in Berlin' (79–94; 2nd edn., 75–87).

[vii] 'Zwei erfolgreiche Halunken' (95–107; 2nd edn., 88–99).

Italian: 'Norimberga per i compagni che sbagliarono', tr. Andrea Affaticati, *Corriere della Sera*, 30 September 1990, 5.

[viii] 'Die Ahnenforscherin' (108–19; 2nd edn., 115–23).

[ix] 'Gibt es zwei deutsche Kulturen? Die Kühlschranktheorie und andere Vermutungen' (120–56; 2nd edn., 124–53).

Italian: 'Fratelli tedeschi. Separati alla nascita'/'Ecco gli Stati Uniti di Germania', *Corriere della Sera*, 15 July 1990, 1–2.

English: 'When the Two Germanies Unite, What Happens to the Bavarian Yodeler?', tr. Eileen Baum, *New York Times Magazine*, 16 September 1990, 41, 44, 105-6.

[x] 'Was wäre, wenn die Mauer fällt' (1st edn. only: 157–76).

[xi] 'Überprüfung eines Szenarios' (1st edn. only: 177–82).
Additional material for 2nd edn.:
[xii] 'Voraussagen und Geschichte' (7–12).
[xiii] 'Ödipus hatte keinen Rechtsanwalt' (100–6).
[xiv] 'Meine Geheimdiensttheorie' (107–14).
[xv] 'Der Vereinigungsschmerz' (154–60).
[xvi] 'Drei schlechte und zwei gute Gründe, die Deutschen zu fürchten' (161–88).
[xvii] 'Mauerhunde' (189–94).
English: 'Berlin: If Dogs Run Free. A Few Last Tails About The Wall' [excerpt from 'Of Dogs and Germans', in *The German Comedy*, 207–12], tr. Philip Boehm, *Harper's Magazine*, 283 No. 1697 (October 1991), 30, 32–5.
Danish: *Den tyske Komedie: scener fra livet efter muren*, tr. Jan Hansen (Copenhagen, Rosinante, 1991).
English: *The German Comedy: Scenes of Life After the Wall*, tr. Philip Boehm and Leigh Hafrey (New York, Farrar, Straus & Giroux, 1991 ('Noonday Books', 1992); London, I.B. Tauris, 1992).
French: *L'allemagne dans tous ses états*, tr. Nicole Casanova (Paris, Grasset, 1991).
Dutch: *Het uiterste midden. Een reis door het duitse nationalisme*, tr. Frans Hille (Houten, De Haan/Unieboek, 1992).
Italian: *Dopo il muro. I volti della nuova Germania*, tr. Umberto Gandini (Milan, Sperling und Kupfer, 1992).
Japanese: [*Extreme Mittellage*], (Tokyo, Chuokoron-Sha, 1992).
Swedish: *Efter muren: en resa genom ten tyska nationalkänslan*, tr. Lars W. Freij (Stockholm, Norstedts, 1992).
[b] 'Mein Sprachrohr' and 'Sechzehn Jahre sind genug. Redeentwurf von Peter Schneider für Willy Brandt', in Klaus Roehler and Rainer Nitsche (eds.), *Das Wahlkontor deutscher Schriftsteller in Berlin 1965. Versuch einer Parteinahme* (Berlin, :TRANSIT, 1990), 89–91 and 92–6.
[c] 'Was heißt jetzt noch Sozialismus? Rede beim Kulturtreff in der Ostberliner Akademie der Künste', *Süddeutsche Zeitung*, 10 (13–14 January), 190.
[d] [interview], *L'Unità*, 19 January. Original version published as '"Es riecht nach östlichem Elend". Der Westberliner Schriftsteller Peter Schneider hält die deutsche Vereinigung für unvermeidbar und Marx' Kritik am Kapitalismus für wichtiger denn je', *die tageszeitung*, 3013 (22 January), 10.
[e] 'Berlin über Berlin unter. Deutsche Szenen, deutsche Zustände', *Die Zeit*, 7 (9 February), 62. Longer revised version reprinted (as 'West-Östliche Passagen') in *Extreme Mittellage* (1990a), 13–32.
Danish: 'Betonrusen. Om Berlinmurens fald', tr. Birgitte Brix, *Fredag*, 5 No. 25 (March 1990), 8, 10–15.

English: 'Concrete and Irony: What the Germans Found When the Wall Came Down', tr. Elliott Rabin, *Harper's Magazine*, 280 No. 1679 (April 1990), 52–6.

Turkish: 'Berlin Aşaği Berlin Yukari. Almanya 'dan Sahneler', in Füsun Ant (ed.), *Almanya Nereye Gidujor?* (Istanbul, AFA, 1990), 23–45.

[f] 'Wir Deutschen rechnen nur noch', *Frankfurter Rundschau*, 68 (21 March), 13.

[g] 'Is Anyone German Here? A Journey into Silesia', tr. Leigh Hafrey, *New York Times Magazine*, 15 April, 28ff. Original version published as 'Reise durch das deutsche Nationalgefühl' in *Extreme Mittellage* (1990a), 33–53.

[h] 'Man kann sogar ein Erdbeben verpassen. Plädoyer für eine Vergangenheitsbewältigung der Linken', *Die Zeit*, 18 (27 April), 57–8. Longer versions reprinted in: *German Politics and Society*, 20 ('Germany: From Plural to Singular': Summer 1990), 1–21 (as 'Man kann ein Erdbeben auch verpassen'); *Extreme Mittellage* (1990a), 54–78 (as 'Man kann sogar ein Erdbeben verpassen').

Italian: 'Si può anche non accorgersi di un terremoto', tr. Luisa Dose, *Nuovi Argomenti*, 35 (July–September 1990), 40–52.

French: 'Comment un tremblement de terre peut passer inaperçu', tr. Nicole Casanova, *La règle du jeu*, 1 No. 2 (September 1990), 203–24.

[i] 'Der Utopie zuliebe – total verrannt. Über Amnesien eines DDR-Dichters', *die tageszeitung*, 3118 (29 May), 10.

[j] [Interventions], in '40 Jahre kann man nicht einfach wegschmeißen' [excerpt from panel discussion ('40 Jahre deutsch-deutsche Literatur – Versuch einer Bilanz') between P.S., Christa Wolf, Karl Mickel, Jurek Becker, Dieter Schlenstedt and Wolfgang Emmerich, held 10 June 1990 in der Akademie der Künste, East Berlin], *Die Volkszeitung*, 25 (15 June), 9.

[k] '"In Deutschland hat Saigon gesiegt". Vietnamesen in Berlin', *Die Zeit*, 27 (29 June). Longer version reprinted with minor revisions in *Extreme Mittellage* (1990a), 79–94.

[l] 'Die Ahnenforscherin', *Kursbuch*, 101 (September 1990), 132–9. Reprinted in *Extreme Mittellage* (1990a), 108–19.

[m] '"Den Fragehorizont offenhalten" – Über deutsche intellektuelle Verarbeitungs- und Verdrängungsstrategien beim Thema "Faschismus". Ein Gespräch mit Peter Schneider am 20.12.89' [interview with Karlheinz Fingerhut], *Diskussion Deutsch*, 21 (1990), 424–33.

1991

[a] *Wie die Spree in den Bosphorus fließt. Briefe zwischen Istanbul und Berlin 1990/1991* (with Aras Ören) (Berlin, Babel Verlag Hund und Toker ('Berliner Edition')).

[b] 'Stranieri, non lasciateci soli con i tedeschi. Intervista a Peter Schneider' [interview with Sandro Pirovano, held October 1990], in Sandro Pirovano, *Berlino*, 2nd edn. (Milan, CittàStudi ('Clup-Guide')), 27–36.

[c] 'Das falsche gute Gewissen der Friedensbewegung. Die deutsche
Öffentlichkeit im Golfkrieg – Skrupellose Händlermentalität und
pazifistische Verblendung – Warum die Regierung schwieg und die
Demonstranten Israel vergaßen', *Frankfurter Allgemeine Zeitung*, 91 (19
April), 36. Revised version reprinted (as part of 'Drei schlechte und zwei
gute Gründe, die Deutschen zu fürchten', 161–88) in *Extreme Mittellage*,
2nd edn. (1992), 180–8.

[d] 'Wider die deutsche Rechthaberei', *Süddeutsche Zeitung*, 92 (20–21
April), 10.

[e] 'Die Angst der Deutschen vor den Idealen. Warum die vergrößerte
Bundesrepublik sich nicht in ihrem politischen Schrebergarten
verstecken kann', *Frankfurter Allgemeine Zeitung*, 109 (13 May), 33–4.
Revised version reprinted (as part of 'Drei schlechte und zwei gute
Gründe, die Deutschen zu fürchten', 161–88) in *Extreme Mittellage*, 2nd
edn. (1992).

[f] 'Belated Marriage', tr. Leigh Hafrey, *Time* (International Edn.), 137 No.
26 (1 July 1991), 36. Longer original version published as 'Der
Vereinigungsschmerz', in *Extreme Mittellage*, 2nd edn. (1992), 154–60.

[g] 'Die Mauer im Kopf', *Frankfurter Allgemeine Zeitung*, 186 (13 August), 21.
Reprinted (as 'Mauerhunde') in *Extreme Mittellage*, 2nd edn. (1992),
189–94.

[h] 'Facing Germany's Newer Past', tr. Leigh Hafrey, *New York Times*, 30
September, Section A, 17ff.

[i] 'Weil er keinen Anwalt hatte, blendete sich Ödipus. Wie soll es mit den
Stasi-Verdächtigungen weitergehen?', *Frankfurter Allgemeine Zeitung*, 249
(26 October), 29. Reprinted (as 'Ödipus hatte keinen Rechtsanwalt') in
Extreme Mittellage, 2nd edn. (1992), 100–6.
Italian: 'Nessuna amnistia per i carnefici', tr. Giuseppina Oneto, *La
Repubblica*, 4 December 1991, 31.

[j] 'In jedem Engagement steckt Narzißmus, dessen Kränkung droht', *die
tageszeitung*, 3555 (8 November), 12.

1992

[a] *Paarungen. Roman* (Berlin, Rowohlt (1994: 'rororo' 13493 (August);
'rororo' 13811 ('Sonderausgabe', October))).
Swedish: *Parningslekar*, tr. Lars W. Freij (Stockholm, Norstedts, 1993).
Danish: *Parforhold*, tr. Jan Hansen (Copenhagen, Munksgaard Rosinante,
1994).
Dutch: *Paren*, tr. Gerrit Bussink (Baarn, De Prom, 1994).
Finnish: *Parisuhteita*, tr. Markku Mannila (Helsinki, Otava, 1994).
French: *La ville des séparations*, tr. Nicole Casanova (Paris, Grasset, 1994).
Italian: *Accoppiamen*, tr. Lidia Castellani (Milan, Garzanti, 1994).

[b] 'Ein Land zum Auswandern', in Bahman Nirumand (ed.), *Angst vor den
Deutschen. Terror gegen Ausländer und der Zerfall des Rechtsstaates*
(Reinbek, Rowohlt ('rororo aktuell' 13176)), 91–9.

[c] 'Wer hier die Fremden sind. Über den Ausländerhaß in Deutschland',
Die Zeit, 2 (3 January), 39.

French: 'La Haine à double tranchant', *Libération*, 17 January 1992, 27.

[d] 'Odiare I Padri e i diversi', *Corriere della Sera*, 117 No. 18 (22 January),
1, 3.

[e] 'Die Staatssicherheit der DDR war ein Riesen-Flop. Wider den Mythos
vom perfekten Geheimdienst', *Frankfurter Rundschau*, 29 February, 'Zeit
und Bild', 2. Longer revised version reprinted (as 'Meine Geheimdiensttheorie') in *Extreme Mittellage*, 2nd edn. (1992), 107–14.

French: 'Le Flop de la Stasi', tr. Emmanuele Peyret, *Libération*, 21
February 1992, 27.

Italian: 'Fede cieca. Nel complotto'/'Servizi segreti? Ma funzionano
meglio quelli postali', tr. Andrea Affaticati, *Corriere della Sera*, 1 March
1992, 1–2.

[f] 'Voices of Europe: Need for Germany far outweighs any fears' [response
to question: 'What effect will German power have on individual
European countries and on Europe itself?'], *New York Times*, 29
September, Section A, 10ff.

[g] 'Contra. Peter Schneider' [response to question: 'Deutsche Not. Für und
wider das Hamburger Manifest: Soll das Asylrecht (Artikel 16)
unverändert bleiben?'], *Die Zeit*, 46 (6 November), 60.

[h] 'Senza Muro e con la crisi "l'essere tedeschi" riempie il vuoto dei valori'
[interview with Guido Olimpio], *Corriere della Sera*, 9 November, 3.

1993

[a] 'Peter Schneider im Gespräch mit Colin Riordan, Berlin, 24. Juni 1990'
[interview on *Vati*], in Colin Riordan (ed.), *Peter Schneider: Vati*
(Manchester, Manchester University Press ('Manchester German Texts');
New York, St Martin's Press), 89–90.

[b] '"Gefangen in der Geschichte". Peter Schneider über das Lagerdenken
der Intellektuellen im Streit um Deutschland und den Fremdenhaß', *Der
Spiegel*, 3 (18 January), 156–7, 160, 162. Revised version reprinted (as
'Wenn die Wirklichkeit die Ideen verrät') in *Vom Ende der Gewißheit*
(1994a), 7–20.

[c] 'Das große Zögern. Die Deutschen erklären sich den Rassenhaß gern,
anstatt ihn zu bekämpfen', *Badische Zeitung*, 17 (22 January), 6. Longer
revised version reprinted in: Bahman Nirumand (ed.), *Deutsche Zustände.
Dialog über ein gefährdetes Land* (Reinbek, Rowohlt ('rororo aktuell'
13354), 1993), 44–51 (as 'Rassismus und Erklärungssucht'); *Vom Ende der
Gewißheit* (1994a), 21–31 (as 'Gewalt und Erklärungssucht').

English: excerpt published as 'Neo-Nazi Violence: Stop it Now, Explain
it Later', tr. Timothy Sultan, *Harper's Magazine*, 286 No. 1717 (June 1993),
20–2.

[d] 'Zehn Thesen gegen schlechte Stimmung in schwieriger Lage. Der
Berliner Schriftsteller Peter Schneider kritisiert den feigen Umgang mit

der riesigen Aufgabe "Deutsche Einheit"', *Berliner Zeitung*, 47 (25 February), 34.

[e] "'Um Himmels willen, nehmt euch Zeit". Peter Schneider über Chancen und Risiken beim Umbau der Hauptstadt Berlin', *Der Spiegel*, 21 (24 May), 54–5, 58–9, 61, 63; *Der Spiegel*, 22 (31 May), 40–1, 44, 47, 50.

[f] 'Serbian Barbarism – And Ours', tr. Leigh Hafrey, *New York Times*, 30 May, Section 4, 11. Longer original version published as 'Bosnien oder Die Lehren der Geschichte' in *Vom Ende der Gewißheit* (1994a), 57–64.

[g] 'Das Kollektiv als Wille & Vorstellung. 20 Jahre Rotbuch-Verlag', *Frankfurter Rundschau*, 132 (11 June), 10.

[h] 'Was ist uns die Zivilisation wert? Überlegungen zu einer europäischen Intervention in Bosnien', *Süddeutsche Zeitung*, 131 (11 June), 13.

[i] 'Es will dich hier niemand ausgrenzen, Arno!', *Frankfurter Allgemeine Zeitung*, 207 (7 September), 37. Longer revised versions reprinted in: *Kursbuch*, 113 ('Deutsche Jugend': September 1993), 131–41 (as 'Erziehung nach Mölln); *Vom Ende der Gewißheit* (1994a), 33–56 (as 'Vom dünnen Firnis der Zivilisation'). Excerpt reprinted (as 'Gewalttäter sind keine Opfer! Statt sie zu entschuldigen, muß sich unsere Gesellschaft endlich gegen sie wehren') in *Das Beste aus Reader's Digest*, 47 No. 1 (1 January 1994), 63–4.

[j] 'Das Volk, das belogen werden will. Peter Schneider: Ein kurzes deutsches Märchen über Kinderverstand und entschlossenes Wegschauen' ['Der Schriftsteller hielt diese Rede am 3.10. auf einer Diskussionsveranstaltung über die "Leistungsfähigkeit der Politik" in Berlin'], *die tageszeitung*, 4138 (15 October), 10.

[k] 'Zukunft ohne Gegenwart. Der Berliner Schriftsteller Peter Schneider über die neueste Lage in seiner Stadt', *Stern*, 8, 94, 98.

1994

[a] *Vom Ende der Gewißheit*. Berlin, Rowohlt. Includes:
[i] 'Wenn die Wirklichkeit die Ideen verrät', 7–20. French: 'Pitié pour les intellectuels', tr. Catherine Weinzorn, *Les Temps Modernes*, 49 No. 575 (June 1994), 36–52.
[ii] 'Gewalt und Erklärungssucht', 21–31.
[iii] 'Vom dünnen Firnis der Zivilisation', 33–56.
[iv] 'Bosnien oder Die Lehren der Geschichte', 57–64.
[v] 'Sarajevo oder Der kurze Weg in die Barbarei', 65–79.
[vi] 'Der Wettlauf um die Unschuld', 81–96.
English: 'Invasions and Evasions', tr. Leigh Hafrey, *New York Times*, 7 June 1994, section A, 23ff. Italian: 'Dalla terra dei colpevoli', tr. Giuseppina Oneto, *La Repubblica*, 131 (7 June 1994), 26. French: 'Les héros oubliés', tr. Pierre Deshusses, *Le Monde des débats*, September 1994.
[vii] 'Die Intellektuellen als Grenzschützer', 97–120.

[b] 'Erziehung nach Mölln', in Heinrich von Berenberg and Klaus Wagenbach (eds.), *Kopfnuss 2. Essays über Kultur und Politik* (Berlin, Wagenbach ('Wagenbachs Taschenbücher' 232)), 77–90.

[c] 'Verschwörung' ['Der Text entstand im Umkreis des Romans *Paarungen*. Das Kapitel wurde nicht in die Endfassung aufgenommen'] and ['Brief an Hartmut Steinecke'], in Hartmut Steinecke (ed.), *Literarisches aus erster Hand. 10 Jahre Paderborner Gast-Dozentur für Schriftsteller* (Paderborn, Igel), 103–7 and 115.

[d] 'Die Mathematik des Todes. Wie soll man eines Tages erklären, warum es den Weltmächten nicht gelang, einem Psychopathen in den Arm zu fallen? Und wer wird in Sarajevo noch leben, um die Erklärung zu hören?', *die tageszeitung*, 4219 (21 January), 9.

[e] 'Der Sündenfall Europas. Peter Schneider über die Massaker von Sarajevo und die Heuchelei des Westens', *Der Spiegel*, 7 (14 February), 140–1, 144, 146. Revised version reprinted (as 'Sarajevo oder Der kurze Weg in die Barbarei') in *Vom Ende der Gewißheit* (1994a), 65–79.

[f] 'Die neuen Kameraden. Eine Meisterleistung der Vereinigung: Wie die NVA aufgelöst wurde', *Der Spiegel*, 24 (13 June), 74–5, 77, 79, 82–3, 87, 89.

[g] 'Der neue deutsche Grobian. Der Schriftsteller Peter Schneider über die wachsende Verrohung der politischen Debatte', *Der Spiegel*, 32 (8 August), 165–70. Longer revised version reprinted (as 'Die Intellektuellen als Grenzschützer') in *Vom Ende der Gewißheit* (1994a), 97–120.

[h] 'Zivilfeigheit', *die tageszeitung*, 8 October, 10.

Selected Secondary Works

The following is a selected bibliography of some of the more substantial contributions to the secondary literature on Peter Schneider. For a more comprehensive bibliography of secondary works (especially reviews), see Buselmeier.

Susan C. Anderson, 'Walls and Other Obstacles: Peter Schneider's Critique of Unity in *Der Mauerspringer*', *German Quarterly*, 66 No. 3 (Summer 1993), 362–71.

Maximilian A. E. Aue, 'Systematische Innerlichkeit. Überlegungen zu Georg Büchners und Peter Schneiders "Lenz"', *Sprachkunst*, 15 No. 1 (1984), 68–80.

Italo Michele Battafarno, 'Zweimal Italien: Peter Schneiders *Lenz* (1973) und Günter Herburgers *Capri* (1984)', *Amsterdamer Beiträge zur neueren Germanistik*, 25 (1988), 235–59.

Manfred Beller, 'Lenz in Arkadien. Peter Schneiders Italienbild von Süden betrachtet', *Arcadia*, 13 (1978), 91–105.

Anna Brychan, 'Yng nghysgod y mur. Gwaith Peter Schneider', *Barn*, 371–2 (December 1993–January 1994), 62–5.

Gordon Burgess, '"Was da ist, das ist (nicht) mein": The Case of Peter Schneider', in Arthur Williams, Stuart Parkes and Roland Smith (eds.), *Literature on the Threshold: The German Novel in the 1980s* (Providence, Oxford and Munich, Berg, 1990), 107–22.

——, 'Büchner, Schneider and Lenz: Two Authors in Search of a Character', in Ken Mills and Brian Keith-Smith (eds.), *Georg Büchner: Tradition and Innovation. Fourteen Essays* (Lewiston, NY, Mellen, 1990), 207–26.

Michael Buselmeier, 'Peter Schneider', in Heinz Ludwig Arnold (ed.), *Kritisches Lexikon zur deutschsprachigen Gegenwartsliteratur* (Munich, text + kritik, 1978ff.), vol. 6, 38 Nlg. (1991), 1–12 + bibliography, A-H.

Manfred Durzak, 'Das Zeitgefühl der Unruhe: Die siebziger Jahre', in *Die deutsche Kurzgeschichte der Gegenwart. Autorenporträts, Werkstattsgespräche, Interpretationen* (Stuttgart, Reclam, 1980), 412–24.

Karlheinz Fingerhut, 'Das Lebensziel: "Nicht so zu werden wie ihre Väter". Zu Peter Schneiders Erzählung "Vati"', *Diskussion Deutsch*, 21 (1990), 416–23.

Karl-Heinz Goetze, 'Gedächtnis. Romane über die Studentenbewegung', *Das Argument*, 23 (1981), 367–82.

Axel Goodbody, 'Walls in the Mind: Peter Schneider and the German Question in the 1980s', *Quinquereme. New Studies in Modern Languages*, 13 (1990–91), 94–109.

Goetz Grossklaus, 'West-östliche Unbehagen. Literarische Gesellschaftskritik in Ulrich Plenzdorfs "Die neuen Leiden des jungen W." und Peter Schneiders "Lenz"', *Basis*, 5 (1975), 80–99.

Klaus Hartung, 'Die Repression wird zum Milieu. Die Beredsamkeit linker Literatur – Peter Schneider, Peter O. Chotjewitz, Inga Buhmann und Bernward Vesper', *Literaturmagazin*, 11 (1979), 52–79.

Adolf Höfer, 'Vater-Sohn-Konflikte in moderner Dichtung. Symptome einer Verharmlosung des Faschismus am Beispiel von Peter Schneiders Erzählung *Vati*', *literatur für leser* (1994) No. 1, 11–22.

Rolf Hosfeld and Helmut Peitsch, '"Weil uns diese Aktionen innerlich verändern, sind sie politisch". Bemerkungen zu vier Romanen über die Studentenbewegung', *Basis*, 8 (1978), 92–126.

Karen Ruoff Kramer, '"New Subjectivity": Third Thoughts on a Literary Discourse', PhD Diss., 1984.

Peter Labanyi, 'When Wishing Still Helped: Peter Schneider's Left-Wing Melancholy', in Keith Bullivant (ed.), *After the 'Death' of Literature: West German Writing of the 1970s* (Providence, Oxford and Munich, Berg, 1989), 313–39.

Peter Laemmle, 'Büchners Schatten. Kritische Überlegungen zur Rezeption von Peter Schneiders "Lenz"', *Akzente*, 21 No. 4 (1974), 469–78.

Edward Larkey, _Literatur der Studentenbewegung. Versuch einer Begriffsbestimmung anhand von Peter Schneiders Erzählung "Lenz"_ (Magisterarbeit, Marburg, 1978).

Manfred Lefèvre, 'Literatur und Politik. Peter Schneider und der "Fall Gorki"', _Berliner Hefte_, 1977 No. 3, 124–32.

Jürgen Lieskounig, 'Der Kampf um die bedrohte Körperlichkeit. Zur Körperwahrnehmung in Werken von Peter Schneider, Verena Stefan und Nicolas Born', _Diskussion Deutsch_, 19 (1988), 279–91.

Timm Reiner Menke, _Lenz-Erzählungen in der deutschen Literatur_ (Hildesheim and Zurich, Olms, 1984).

Peter Morgan, 'The Sins of the Fathers: A Reappraisal of the Controversy about Peter Schneider's _Vati_', _German Life and Letters_, 47 No. 1 (January 1994), 104–33.

Leslie Morris, 'Aesthetic, Political or Anti-Idyll: "Das Italien-Erlebnis" in Works by Christine Wolter, Birgit Pausch and Peter Schneider', _Neue Germanistik_, 4 No. 2 (Spring 1986), 13–23.

Helmut Peitsch, 'Die problematische Entdeckung nationaler Identität. Westdeutsche Literatur am Beginn der 80er Jahre', _Diskussion Deutsch_, 18 (1987), 373–92.

Malcolm Pender, 'Historical Awareness and Peter Schneider's _Lenz_', _German Life and Letters_, 37 No. 2 (1984) , 150–60.

Wilhelm Heinrich Pott, 'Über den fortbestehenden Widerspruch von Politik und Leben. Zur Büchner-Rezeption in Peter Schneiders Erzählung "Lenz"', in Ludwig Fischer (ed.), _Zeitgenosse Büchner_ (Stuttgart, Klett-Cotta, 1979), 96–130.

Colin Riordan, 'Introduction', in Colin Riordan (ed.), _Peter Schneider: Vati_ (Manchester, Manchester University Press; New York, St Martin's Press, 1993), 1–31.

Ivar Sagmo, 'Vom anderen Gesetz im ähnlichen Leben. Fremderfahrungen in und mit Peter Schneiders Erzählung _Der Mauerspringer_', _Jahrbuch Deutsch als Fremdsprache_, 11 (1985), 191–202.

Oskar Sahlberg, 'Peter Schneiders Lenz-Figur', in Ludwig Fischer (ed.), _Zeitgenosse Büchner_ (Stuttgart, Klett-Cotta, 1979), 131–52.

Irmela Schneider, 'Zerrissenheit als Geschichtserfahrung. Überlegungen zu Georg Büchners _Lenz_, einer Erzählung von Peter Schneider und einem Roman von Nicholas Born', _Text und Kontext_, 12 No. 1 (1984), 43–63.

Michael Schneider, 'Die Linke und die Neue Sensibilität', in _Die lange Wut zum langen Marsch_ (Reinbek, Rowohlt, 1975), 304–34.

Gisela Shaw, '"Die Mauer im Kopf": Observations on Peter Schneider's _Der Mauerspringer_', _New German Studies_, 11 No. 3 (Autumn 1983), 191–201.

——, 'Peter Schneider und Berlin. Die Suche nach einem Standort', _Modern German Studies_, 5 (August 1988), 42–51.

Ibuki Shitahodo, 'Büchners und Peter Schneiders "Lenz". Ein vergleichender Versuch in Sicht der heutigen Büchner-Rezeption', _Forschungsberichte zur Germanistik_, 22 (1980), 59–75.

Thomas Steinfeld and Heidrun Suhr, 'Die Wiederkehr des Nationalen: Zur Diskussion um das deutschlandpolitische Engagement in der Gegenwartsliteratur', *The German Quarterly*, 62 (1989), 345-56.

Zbigniew Swiatłowski, 'Die befragte Geschichte. Die Modifikationen der "politischen Prosa" in den siebziger Jahren', *Germanica Wratslaviensia*, 55 (1984), 59–72.

Andrzej Talarczyk, 'Rückkehr der persönlich erlittenen Widersprüche in Peter Schneiders "Lenz"', *Studia i Materialy Germanistika*, 2 (1986), 59–74.

Waltraud Wende-Hohenberger, 'Die verschmähte "Gnade der späten Geburt". Versuche literarischer Vergangenheitsbewältigung bei Jurek Becker, Gert Heidenreich und Peter Schneider', *Das Argument*, 29 (1987), 44–9.

Herbert Wiesner, 'Geteilte Ansichten oder Das langsame Abreißen der Mauer im Kopf', *Lesezeichen*, 1982 No. 4 (March).

Kangkang Zhang, 'Betrachtungen eines Marsmenschen über einen Erdenmenschen. In Erinnerung an Peter Schneider', tr. Christoph Palm, *Zeitschrift für Kulturaustausch*, 36 (1986), 328–32.

Index